About the Author

Duncan Bannatyne is one of Britain's best-known entrepreneurs thanks to his appearances on *Dragons' Den*. A regular investor in new companies, he is chairman of the Bannatyne Group, which owns and operates hotels, health clubs, spas and bars. In 2011, the *Sunday Times* Rich List estimated his personal worth at £430 million, having started his business career with an investment of £450 in an ice-cream van. His first book, *Anyone Can Do It*, was a *Sunday Times* bestseller in both hardback and paperback and has sold in excess of 200,000 copies. He has six children, and homes in London, the North East of England and the south of France.

Duncan's blog can be found at www.bannatyne.co.uk or you can follow him on Twitter at twitter.com/duncanbannatyne

Jo Monroe, who has worked with Duncan Bannatyne on all his books, is a ghostwriter and journalist who has written for *The Times*, the *Guardian* and *Time Out*.

Her website is www.jomonroe.com

Also by Duncan Bannatyne and available from Headline:

43 Mistakes Businesses Make . . . and How to Avoid Them

DUNCAN BANNATYNE

37 Questions Everyone in Business Needs to Answer

headline

business plus

First published in Great Britain in 2012 by
HEADLINE PUBLISHING GROUP

1

Cataloguing in Publication Data is available from the British Library

ISBN 978 0 7553 6239 4

Typeset in Stone Serif by Avon DataSet Ltd,
Bidford-on-Avon, Warwickshire

Printed and bound in Great Britain by
Clays Ltd, St Ives, Suffolk

Headline's policy is to use papers that are natural, renewable and
recyclable products and made from wood grown in sustainable
forests. The logging and manufacturing processes are expected to
conform to the environmental regulations of the country of origin.

HEADLINE PUBLISHING GROUP
An Hachette UK Company
338 Euston Road
London NW1 3BH

www.headline.co.uk
www.hachette.co.uk

To Abigail, Hollie, Jennifer, Eve, Emily and Tom.
Remember, I love you more . . .

Acknowledgements

First and foremost I would like to thank my children Abigail, Hollie, Jennifer, Eve, Emily and Tom, as well as my grand-children Ava and Austin. Thank you and I love you all so much.

I would like to thank Jo Monroe for working with me for a sixth time; it has been an absolute pleasure. Thanks also to John Moseley, Jonathan Taylor and the team at Headline Publishing and Jonny Geller at Curtis Brown; your help with this book has been invaluable.

A big thank you to everyone.

Contents

Introduction

Anyone who has seen *Dragons' Den* will know that the way we analyse an investment is by asking questions – what's the profit, what are the projections, who are the main rivals, and so on. Given the popularity of the show, I'm surprised how few people have realised that it's not just investors who should be asking these questions. Whether you run your own company or are employed by someone else, asking some Dragon-style questions about the state of your business will help you maximise your return, or plot the fastest route to the top.

The questions in this book are designed to help you analyse the strengths and weaknesses of your business and your industry, as well as yourself. If you want to know why you're not making much in the way of profits, or are stuck in a mid-ranking position, then figuring out honest answers to these questions will help you understand why. Once you've come up with your answers, you'll be able to start making changes that will transform your working life.

It doesn't matter if your career started 20 years ago or 20 days ago, we should all be asking ourselves the same questions: where are the opportunities, am I getting paid enough, who should I be working with, what's the next big thing? Whether you want to impress the boss or you are the boss, the questions in this book are designed to help you get the most out of every working day.

Duncan Bannatyne
March 2012

QUESTION

What's my bestselling line?

IT'S AMAZING HOW MANY BUSINESS OWNERS AND departmental managers can't answer this question. It doesn't matter whether you're in retail or the service sector, every business sells things and if you want your business to succeed, you need to know what you sell the most of.

Take my hotel business as an example. I need to know if I sell more weekend breaks or more midweek breaks. I also need to know if I sell more chicken or fish dinners in our restaurants. And in our spas, I need to know if people are ordering more massages or more manicures. Why do I need to know these things? Because if I can work out why one product is selling better than another, then I can use that information to a) sell more of it, but b) sell more of everything else too.

To work out your bestselling line, you first have to get hold of accurate sales figures for each of your products and/or services. It's amazing how many businesses never bother to find this information out, relying instead on hunches and anecdotes. It's usually because they don't have the right systems in place for collecting the data, which means getting accurate figures is so time-consuming they never bother. Their sales data sits on individual desks or computers and is never properly collated. Or they might have an order book and a sales chart but never compare the two. Every manager has their sales data somewhere in their system but some have to look harder for it than others. Which means that if you run or are employed by a business that doesn't harvest and process this kind of data properly, you can engineer an easy win for yourself by being the person who puts new data-collection systems in place. If you become the person who collects this information, you will find you soon have a great deal of power within your organisation.

Analysing the data

Once you've got your sales data, you need to analyse it to work out why one line sells better than another. Generally, consumers make their purchases based on one of four things: price, quality, service and convenience. However, other factors like fashion, branding, money-off coupons or a persuasive sales pitch can also make a difference. You need to scrutinise the data to look for correlations between your sales figures and other factors. For instance, look to see if there is a relationship between a recent advertising campaign and an uptake in demand, or if certain products sell well in certain price brackets. Perhaps you're selling more of something because it is prominently displayed, either on your home page or on your shop floor. Depending on your business, you might also look to see if you sell more at the end of the month, or the beginning of the day, or during the school holidays.

Your data should also tell you how you get most of your sales – online, in person, over the phone, or maybe through an affiliate. This can help you target your resources to clinch future sales, and the further you burrow down into the data, the more information you'll find to help increase sales. The more data you collect, the more useful it will be: gathering sales figures over time lets you spot trends and can tell you if you're selling more of a particular product than you did this time last year, or if your sales are declining.

Once you've spotted these patterns and correlations, the next step is to ask yourself why your sales data is telling you these things. The correlation between an advertising campaign and a spike in sales is pretty bloody obvious, but other factors might take a little detective work to uncover. Perhaps the staff who sell your goods and services have been better trained to sell one product over another. Maybe the supplier gives them promotional material that helps them close a sale, maybe one offers better value to the end user, or maybe your sales team use the product personally and their passion for it shines through when they talk to customers.

There is one extraordinarily simple way to find out why your customers choose one product over another – and that's to ask them. Consumers have got used to being asked for feedback. *Where did you hear about us? Who helped you with your purchase today?* It doesn't matter whether you ask your customers in a formal questionnaire, or if you get your sales team to ask them why they've chosen a particular product at the point of sale, or whether you just call up a handful of key clients and ask them for their thoughts: it only matters that you ask.

Using the data

Once you've found out why customers buy certain products, you need to start putting the information you've uncovered to good use. If you use the data correctly, your bestselling line will start to sell even better.

For instance, you should now be able to predict with greater accuracy how many of a particular product you will sell at any given time, which means you can look at your stock-control processes and make sure that you never run out of your key product. You can make sure you have the staff in place to deal with demand at key times and that they are trained to deal with enquiries or problems. And if you know you can sell more of a particular product, then you will be in a strong position to negotiate better terms with suppliers, which in turn means you can make more of a profit on each sale.

The data you gather about your bestselling line can also help you boost the sales of other products and services. If your research tells you that better training, or better promotional literature, or a different price bracket has boosted the sales of one product, then it makes sense to apply those techniques to all your products and services. Might a few days of training lead to years of increased sales? Might a small investment in promotional discounts lead to increased enquiries from customers?

Finally, when you look at your sales data, you should also be asking yourself a supplementary question: what's *not* selling? Does your company offer products or services that no one is interested in? Are there goods taking up space in your warehouse that no one wants? Are you training staff to provide manicures when most of your customers want massages? Not only can you maximise your profits on the lines that are selling, but you can use this data to cut your losses on the products that not enough people want.

QUESTION

Who's my successor?

IN 1997, I RECEIVED THE CV OF A YOUNG ACCOUNTANT called Nigel Armstrong. He hadn't passed all the exams needed to become a chartered accountant, but he had worked for another local entrepreneur and his covering letter said he was looking for an opportunity to do more than crunch numbers. I invited him in for a chat and ended up offering him the position of financial controller in my new health club business. I could have told you back then that Nigel had a long-term future at Bannatyne Fitness: after 14 years of hard work and dedication, he's now our chief executive.

The issue of succession is vitally important to businesses. If all your company's talent, contacts and drive come from the same person, the business becomes worthless if that person decides to leave. And if you are the founder of a business where the workforce relies on you for everything, you will never be able to move on without your business suffering. Identifying and mentoring your successor is one of the ways in which you ensure your business continues to flourish. As we'll see shortly, it isn't just entrepreneurs who need to know who will sit at their desk one day – managers need to know this too.

One of the best examples of how important succession is comes from Apple Inc. When Steve Jobs, one of the original founders of Apple, returned to the organisation in 1997, the company was on its knees. Its share price was on the floor, its sales were on the slide and Apple was seen as a niche computer manufacturer for geeks. And then along came the iMac, followed by the iPod. And iTunes and iPhones and iPads and all those Apple stores where hundreds of thousands of customers play with gadgets for hundreds of thousands of hours. Steve Jobs utterly transformed Apple and sent its share price into the stratosphere. And then it was announced that Steve Jobs was ill and was stepping aside while he received treatment for pancreatic cancer. There were many, many commentators who were convinced that Jobs' absence would see the collapse of Apple. It didn't, because the man Jobs had handpicked to take over from him was ready and able to take on the biggest job in technology.

Tim Cook was the chief operating officer of Apple and had been responsible for the day-to-day running of the vast tech giant for years. Cook's firm hand on the tiller had actually enabled Jobs to spend his time as the company's chief visionary, someone who could work with and inspire the developers and programmers to come up with new pro- ducts and software. When Jobs took time off, investors knew that Cook could keep the company running and that there would be a string of innovative products coming to the market.

When Jobs returned to the company after receiving a liver transplant, it was clear from looking at him that he had been incredibly ill. He was gaunt, he was greyer, he was weaker, and there were many people both in and outside the company who assumed he was dying. His return to the top job was only temporary. Everyone knew it, and everyone at Apple prepared for it. So when Steve Jobs stepped down as CEO for a second time in the spring of 2011, the share price hardly moved. Investors, customers and employees knew that while things weren't going well for Jobs, things were doing just fine at Apple. Within a few months of Cook taking over, Apple became the most valuable company on the planet. If Apple had not handled the succession so well, the company could have experienced a different fate at the hands of the stock market when Jobs' death was announced in October 2011.

If I hadn't spotted Nigel Armstrong's abilities and prepared him for the top job, then I wouldn't have time to write books and make TV programmes. And it's not just me who benefits: the rest of the staff do too. They know that if anything happens to me, the business will not suffer. And for businesses that have shareholders, a succession plan for senior members of staff offers their investors security.

There's a reason why so many organisations fail when it comes to succession, and it usually comes down to ego, especially when founders of companies are involved. Most people in positions of power like to think that they are irreplaceable and some even actively push away anyone able enough to be a threat to their authority. Of course, in strengthening their own position, they weaken their company's standing. And if they ever change their mind and decide the time is right to move on, they may very well find they are trapped.

Who should you be looking for?

The ideal person to succeed you in your current role is someone who is better at it than you, because that way you can move on and not worry about what you've left behind. A good and able successor is the person who allows you to fulfil your potential. This is particularly true of managers wanting to move up the career ladder: imagine how much easier it is for your boss to promote you if you both know that your existing role will be filled by the right person.

The ideal candidate to succeed you should be as ambitious for success as you were when you started in the role, and just as passionate about the company as you are. Everything else is up for grabs. They might be better at accounts than you, or sales, or team-building, or they might be worse at those things – what matters is that they have an understanding of why your company, or department, is successful and how that success has been achieved. Whatever skills they lack can be hired in so that your successor is free to lead and play to their strengths, just as you have done.

Companies thrive when they find the right balance between stability and innovation. You don't, therefore, want your successor to be a carbon copy of you, as that would lead to stagnation, but you do want someone who shares enough of your values and attributes so that the company doesn't have the business equivalent of a heart attack. The ideal successor will share enough of your values to ensure ·

continuity, but be sufficiently distinct so that the business keeps moving forward.

In my experience, letting people know that you won't always be around is a great way of motivating them, especially if you are the founder of a company. Put yourself in their shoes: are they going to want to work for a company where their potential will be fulfilled, or one where their ambition will be kept in check by your continued presence in the CEO's chair? You don't have to promise people that you'll step aside and give them your job, but if they know that they might eventually sit at your desk, then you will motivate them and inspire them. I never said to Nigel that he would one day be running the company, but I certainly told him that there would always be opportunities for advancement if he showed the right qualities.

Over the years, I found projects to give Nigel to see how he would get on, and I tested him to make sure that he had the skills and abilities to take on more responsibilities. We both knew that he couldn't become the company's finance director because he didn't have the right accountancy qualifications, so we both looked for opportunities for him to get involved in the general management of the business. In due course, he became the managing director and is now the CEO.

If Nigel hadn't come to work with me, I would have either groomed someone else in the organisation to take on the top job, or I would have kept a close eye on people working in other organisations. If Nigel resigned tomorrow, I know whose number I would call to replace him, because I pay attention when I meet people from other organisations – not just our rival health clubs – and if one of them strikes me as the kind of leader who could keep moving Bannatyne

Fitness forward, then I follow their career very closely.

The reality of modern business is that workforces are highly mobile and the best people will always be headhunted by rivals. And even if you offer them incentives to stay, there will come a time when ambitious people want a change and there will be nothing you can do to hold on to them. The success of your business, therefore, will depend at some point on your ability to appoint the right person to the right job, especially if that job is currently yours.

QUESTION

Who's my biggest rival?

RIVALS ARE REALLY IMPORTANT IN BUSINESS, JUST AS THEY are in sport. Think of local derby football matches: they're usually harder fought and produce more goals. Think of Usain Bolt: his success, in part, is down to the fact that Jamaica has produced so many fast sprinters in the past decade, and every one of them has pushed him to go faster. A good rival is nothing to be afraid of. A good rival is actually your best friend.

At Bannatyne Fitness, it's not always easy to say who our biggest rival is. You might think it's the other fitness operators, like LA Fitness or Esporta, but except in big cities, we're often the only operator in the areas where we have clubs. Local residents are unlikely to drive to another town to use one of their clubs when they can use ours. Nevertheless, I still consider the other operators to be massive rivals, and I study them almost as much as I analyse my own business: if someone has the choice of joining a Bannatyne's club near their home or a rival near their work, then I want to be absolutely sure they will choose us.

One of the simplest ways I rate my rivals is by looking at how much they charge and the value they offer their members. Other simple comparisons are finding out what new equipment they've got, or what offers they're promoting. I do this because I want Bannatyne Fitness to offer the best facilities at the best price for our members. I know that if our standards slacked off or our prices crept up, I might find that some of our members would be prepared to drive to another club. Offering a service that is better than my competitors' is the best way I have of keeping their custom.

Keeping tabs on my rivals ensures Bannatyne Fitness remains competitive, which in turn helps deter other operators from opening in close proximity to me. Equally, if I see that a competitor is failing their members, then I might see an opportunity to open a club on their turf and be confident that I could win over their members.

By knowing my competitors almost as well as I know my own business, I spot trends and opportunities I would miss if I focused solely on Bannatyne Fitness. That's why I don't just follow the fortunes of British health club owners – I know exactly what all the big international gyms have going for them as well, just in case any of them offers a class or piece of equipment that we don't. (And, of course, if any of them ever want to move to the UK, I'll know if I want to merge with them, take them over, or sell to them.)

It's not just the clubs themselves that I compare. I look at my rivals' accounts and balance sheets. If businesses are publicly listed on the Stock Exchange, they have to publish their accounts, and I scrutinise my rivals' figures to see how much money they are making. If they are private companies, then I get their accounts from Companies House. I check to see what their costs and profit margins are because I don't just want Bannatyne Fitness to be the best health club operator in the country, I want it to be the most competitive business in the industry. My innate competitiveness means I want to make more profit – per club, per member, per square foot – than my rivals. This comparison with my rivals helps me run a tighter ship and produce better profits.

The big health club chains aren't my only rivals of course. In every town there are small independent gyms and council-run leisure centres that local residents could use instead of Bannatyne's. Generally, these offer far fewer facilities than we do, and if customers want to make their choice on price alone, then the chances are they will choose the cheaper option. These rivals offer a completely different threat to my business, but I don't see myself as in competition with these providers at all. I don't think you can offer a decent gym membership for £20 a month. If people want basic, then they can have basic. They just won't get it from me. To illustrate this, a few years ago, the former Dragon James Caan invested in a cut-price gym venture called NuYuu that offered membership for £19.99 a month. They opened a branch within a few minutes of my club in Livingstone, but I wasn't worried: I was confident that once customers had tried a £20 club they would see the value of their Bannatyne's membership. I was right not to worry: NuYuu closed within months.

Not all of Bannatyne Fitness's rivals are in the health club sector: I never forget that we compete for the disposable income of our members with all the things they could spend money on – Sky TV, entertainment, holidays, gadgets, going out . . . This is especially true in the current climate, when household incomes are being squeezed. I have to make sure we continue to give our members value for money and afford-able luxury. The point I want to get across is that your biggest rival might not be immediately apparent.

Sometimes entrepreneurs tell me they don't have a rival. 'No one else is offering this service/product/price in this area,' they say. They seem to have forgotten that business is inter-national: companies and households can source their products and services from anywhere in the world at the click of a mouse. If anyone tells you they don't have a rival, then they are deluding themselves.

Let me give you an example. Let's imagine someone who is running a stationery shop. They might think that their biggest rival is the other stationery shop on their high street, especially if that's a branch of Ryman or WHSmith. So long as they are able to stock a better range, or offer better prices, than these high-street rivals, they probably think they'll be able to stay in business. However, their local supermarket sells notepads and copier paper, the toyshop sells pencil cases and craft materials, and the local gallery probably sells wrapping paper and gift cards. And I haven't even mentioned the ink cartridges and office supplies bought in PC World or Staples. Or catalogue retailers like Viking Direct, or the countless online stationery suppliers. Whether they realise it or not, the owner of our imaginary stationery shop has a vast number of very real competitors.

The best example I know of an industry not understanding who its real rival was is the book trade. Fifteen years ago, there was only one way to buy a book – in a shop. Booksellers had to compete with each other to have the best ranges, the best service and the best locations. While independent bookshops were worrying about the threat from chains like Waterstones, Borders and Books Etc, a man called Jeff Bezos was founding Amazon.com. Borders and Books Etc have since disappeared from our high streets, as have many independent bookshops. They just did not see their biggest rival coming until it was too late.

To be fair to those bookshops that have gone under, it's difficult to know how to respond to the threat from as mighty a rival as Amazon, but some are still in business, many of them by selling through Amazon's Marketplace to reach new customers. The moral of the demise of the book trade is to never stop looking for rivals.

The rival at the next desk

Of course, rivalry isn't just an issue between companies: it exists *within* them too. And just like external rivals, you can use the rival at the next desk, or the next branch or office, to spur you on to achieve more. Within Bannatyne Fitness, I set different clubs and different regions targets in the hope and expectation that they will outperform their rivals at neighbouring clubs. Most businesses use internal rivalries to get the most out of their teams, whether it's offering Employee of the Month certificates or bonuses for their top sales executive.

And then, of course, there's the kind of rivalry that happens without any encouragement from the boss: two colleagues trying to outdo each other to impress their manager, or competing for a promotion or to close a sale. It's not always obvious who your rivals are when you start a new job, but it's worth making a close assessment of the people you work with. See if you can work out who's next in line for promotion or a lucrative bonus, and work out why. Not only will you be able to see if they have any habits or skills that you can replicate, but you will also be able to set yourself apart from them: once you've identified your rivals' strengths and weaknesses, it's easier to work out your own. If your rival is good at one thing, you need to work out if you can be better at that task, or if you should specialise in another area. Rivals don't just bring out your competitive side, they also help you to differentiate yourself in the marketplace. And that's as true within a single company as it is within an entire industry: it's by getting to know our rivals that we start to see ourselves more clearly.

QUESTION

4

How much should I be paid?

YOUR ANSWER TO THIS QUESTION DOESN'T JUST AFFECT what you can buy this month; it also has profound consequences for every area of your life. If you spend five years of your career earning £5,000 less than your true earnings potential, that's £25,000 you've missed out on. The amount you earn doesn't just affect the quality of your life in the short term; it affects things like whether or not you can get a mortgage and the amount of money you can borrow to buy a property. That in turn might have an impact on where you choose to live, or whether you move in with your partner, or even how many children you have. Your current income also affects how much money you can set aside for your future, or your children's future. If your first instinct was to answer this question by saying 'not enough', I hope I've persuaded you that this isn't something to be flippant about.

There are also consequences to not earning enough that are harder to quantify. If you feel you are not being paid enough, it's likely that you will be resentful and not get the most out of your working life. You might change jobs more frequently in search of a higher salary, and that may mean that you never get the promotions or make the friendships that come from sticking around in one place for a long time.

If you've not given much thought to whether you're being paid enough before now, I hope by the end of this chapter you'll realise just how important it is to every area of your life that you maximise your income. Unless, that is, you own your own business . . .

Business owners

It's very difficult when you start a business, especially if it's your first business, to know exactly what belongs to the company and what belongs to you. Surely any profit is yours to do with as you wish? Technically that may be the case, but unless you leave a good percentage of the company's profits in the company's bank account, you won't be able to invest in the company or see it through a lean patch. However, it's not easy to know how much of the profit should be yours to keep, and how much should stay in the company's coffers.

I completely understand why so many new entrepreneurs have difficulty deciding how much to pay themselves, and it doesn't help that the tax system actually encourages business owners to take their income in the form of dividends rather than as a salary (as this avoids paying employer's NI contributions on the money). If you sacrifice a decent salary in the anticipation of dividends in the future, you may well feel a sense of entitlement to any profits when your company does well.

The balance business owners need to strike is between short-term income and long-term wealth. If money is paid out to the owner at the expense of investing in the business, then the owner is likely to earn less from the company in the long term, because that business won't be able to grow at the same rate. There are no hard and fast rules about how to get the right balance between the owner's income and the business's profits, but here are the things I think you should consider.

A. How old is the business?

If your business is less than a year old, I think you should be paying yourself the barest minimum. Work out what the minimum you need to survive on is, and make that your income (and don't forget, you will have to pay tax and NI on that). I say this because a) in the first year of a business you will be working so hard that you won't have time to spend your income, and b) you have no idea until you've been trading for at least a year what your costs and earnings are going to be over that year. You might have a big spike in salaries or supplies, or you might have a bumper Christmas and suddenly double your takings. Until you can accurately predict what your annual earnings should be, you should take as little as possible out of the company's coffers. The more established your business, the more confidently you can pay yourself a salary that reflects your true value.

B. Salary v dividends

If you are a business owner, or a shareholder in a business, taking some of your income as dividends (i.e. paying yourself a share of the profit) rather than paying yourself a monthly salary can reduce the amount of money you, and your business, hands over to the Inland Revenue. In the 2011–12 tax year, employers' NIC was 13.8 per cent, and employees' contributions were 12 per cent. What that means is that if your company pays you a gross salary of £25,000, you will make a contribution of around £2,000 a year (once your NI allowance is taken into consideration) and your company will hand over an additional £2,475 after allowances.

We can all earn a certain amount before we start paying tax and NI, and if you pay yourself a salary below this amount (it was approximately £7,500 in 2011–12 and is expected to rise to £10,000 by 2015), then it's even possible you could avoid making any contributions at all. That might sound like a good way to save money, but it's understandably a practice that invites scrutiny from tax inspectors, which is why I'd recommend you get professional help from your accountant or tax adviser before doing this. It's not illegal, but if they suspect that you are evading making contributions, then you can expect to hear from them. I should also point out that this only applies to NI contributions: you will still, of course, have to pay tax on your income, whether you take the dividends or PAYE route.

There is another problem with taking dividends, as you can't really pay them until you know what your annual profit is going to be, which is precisely why most companies pay dividends either annually or every six months. However, most of the bills you will have outside of your business will be monthly or weekly: getting paid in big lump sums might help the business, but it probably won't help your household finances. Receiving a regular salary may be more desirable for you, even if it isn't the most cost-effective way of paying yourself.

Until your company's income and expenditure is secure and predictable, I would recommend that you pay yourself the smallest salary you can survive on, and then take a dividend payment when the business can comfortably afford it.

C. Personal wealth v business wealth

As a general rule, the wealth of the owner and the wealth of the business should be roughly equal. Over the years, I have seen many entrepreneurs driving expensive cars and living in massive houses when their businesses were suffering. Equally, I've known a few people who were too cautious to take money out of their businesses in the good years and missed out on an enviable lifestyle.

If your business regularly produces a profit of £2m a year, then you can happily pay yourself a seven-figure sum. If your business produces a profit of £2m for just one year, then you can safely buy yourself a few treats, but unless a good proportion of that cash is re-invested in the business, the chances of you ever getting that kind of payday again are slim.

Obviously the reason why most people start a business is because they hope it will make them rich, but it's important to remember that big fortunes can only be built on solid foundations. If you take too much money out of your business too soon, there's a good chance it will be to the detriment of your long-term earnings.

Employees

As an employee, you want to know you are being paid the best possible salary in exchange for your labour, your ideas and your commitment. And in all but a handful of situations, the 'best possible' salary is also the highest. Unless your employer is near bankruptcy and paying you more would send the company into receivership, or your employer offers you generous incentives like flexitime or home-working, then you need to be sure you are maximising your salary.

One way to find out how much someone with your experience and expertise should be getting paid is to key in your details into one of the numerous online salary-checkers. Keep in mind that the programs and algorithms used to generate the results are never going to know exactly what experience you have, or precisely how much a company would be willing to pay for your services, but it's a good start. The more mainstream your job is – e.g. bank teller rather than ghostbuster – the more useful the results will be. If the figure you find online differs greatly from your salary, it's useful ammunition for negotiating a better deal with your boss.

While you're online, Google for a 'salary survey' and see if you can find one of the numerous reports the big recruitment agencies publish on salary levels each year. Again, it might not be specific enough for your needs, but you'll find useful figures to know if your income is at least in the right ballpark.

You should also try to get some information from your employer's HR department. Although you're unlikely to be told exactly what your colleagues are being paid, you should be able to find out if your company has specific pay grades for specific jobs. If you've been in the company for a number of years, it's just possible that your salary has not kept pace with what they are paying new recruits, so check your income is within the right pay grade. Just make sure if the figures include bonuses and overtime before you kick up a stink! And, of course, if a similar job to yours is advertised with a much higher salary, then this is perfect ammunition to renegotiate your salary – especially if you successfully apply for the new job and are willing to walk out.

There's one other thing you can do to make sure you are being paid the going rate, and that's to ask your co-workers what their salary is. It's very un-British to reveal what you get paid, but if you do have the kind of relationship with your colleagues where you can ask (and be sure you're getting an honest answer), then this is a sure-fire way of ensuring you're not being underpaid. You can always ask several of them to write a figure down anonymously and put all the bits of paper into a hat.

If these enquiries reveal that you are not being paid enough, then you have the option of either looking for another job that pays better, or negotiating a pay rise. The more ammunition you have, the stronger your case will be, but in the current economic climate, many employers will struggle to increase their staff costs. At a time when redundancies and pay freezes are common, you may have to leave your employer to increase your income.

Every few months, one of my senior managers will come

to me and tell me that they've been headhunted by one of our rivals who are offering them £10,000 more a year. I don't immediately offer to match our rival, as I know there are other reasons beside salary for my staff to choose to work for Bannatyne's. What I say to them is that if they can produce a formal job offer from our rival and give it to me with their resignation letter, then I can decide if I want to match it. Only if people really are prepared to walk will I think about negotiating. I suspect that in the current economic situation, I won't be the only boss that thinks long and hard before offering anyone a pay rise, even the really talented people.

QUESTION

What's the next technological shift?

IT DOESN'T MATTER WHAT INDUSTRY YOU'RE IN, technology will have a massive influence on how you make money. I'm not just talking about iPads and gadgets; I'm talking about things like whether farmers use genetically modified seed or GP surgeries offer automated bookings: every business in every industry is impacted by changes in technology. The important thing to remember is that some businesses benefit from these changes, while others suffer. The way to make sure you come out on top is to anticipate what those changes will be and work out how you can profit from them.

There are loads of examples of businesses suffering because they failed to respond to technological shifts. I've already mentioned how bookshops closed in the face of the Amazonian onslaught, but there are plenty of other, less spectacular failures. In the hotel industry, for example, a few years ago, a B&B or small family hotel that didn't have an online presence saw bookings tumble, and these days an online presence isn't enough – you need to be able to take bookings online and be prepared to share your revenue with sites like Lastminute and Expedia. Unless you move in line with your customers' expectations, your business will suffer. Cast your mind back to the 1990s, when Marks & Spencer was in the doldrums: that, in part, was down to the fact that they didn't accept credit cards! One of the nation's biggest retailers hadn't worked out that a huge percentage of their customers no longer carried chequebooks or wads of cash.

Of course, change costs. If you are upgrading your computer systems to take credit cards, or replacing your machinery on the shop floor, or installing flat-screen TVs in your hotel rooms, it will cost you money. You need to decide if it's prudent to pay that price, or if you will suffer in the long term if you don't make that investment.

Universal trends

The first area to consider is the technological advancements that are reported in the media every day. Things like paying for things with mobile phones, or geolocation software in smart phones, or social networking, or video conferencing, or electric cars, or the switch from analogue TV to digital. Every time you see a technological revolution reported by the media, you should be asking yourself if it will have an impact on your business, or your industry, and why.

The impact these changes will have may not be easy to determine and, at first glance, you may wonder if it will have an impact on your company at all. As an example, let's look at my hotel business – my company owns four hotels and we plan to open several more – and the seemingly unrelated advent of tablet computers. At first, you might think it makes no difference whatsoever, because customers were already booking online and it shouldn't matter one jot to me whether they book via their iPad or their netbook.

But if you examine the impact of tablet computers on my customers, you see just how important mobile computing has become. And not just for business travellers. Everyone expects to be able to check their emails on the move these days, and plenty of parents keep their kids happy by letting them play games on their tablets. And because so many of these devices store apps and documents in 'the cloud' rather than on a hard drive, tablet users are always going to be hungry for wifi access. To sum up then, the impact of tablet computing on my hotel business is that I need to offer a good wifi signal in every room and throughout the hotel. If I don't, I know I will start to lose customers to hotels that do provide such a service.

If you struggle to think how these universal technological shifts will impact on your business, try instead to imagine how it will affect your customers. That should indicate the path you need to take towards the future.

Industrywide trends

I've been running health clubs for 15 years, and in that time I've seen one craze follow another. Yoga was out and Pilates was in. Aerobics was over and spin was suddenly in demand. These days it's zumba that my members want. And with each new trend we need to buy new equipment and train our staff.

When I think about the fitness equipment we had just five years ago, it seems antiquated, and yet I remember thinking that a treadmill that could record your heart rate was really impressive! These days, fitness equipment comes with built-in individual TVs and video games. If health clubs like mine don't keep offering the latest equipment, we give our members a reason to start looking for another club to join.

And it's not just fitness equipment that changes. My members have different expectations: these days, they expect to be able to contact us 24 hours a day, so we now have a helpline and can respond to problems by phone, email or on Twitter. It'll be the same in your industry too: whatever field you're in, there will be changes in technology and customer expectation that you will need to respond to. The companies that can anticipate these changes will be the ones that will thrive.

There are several ways you can keep on top of these innovations. You can read the trade papers for your industry, attend conferences and events where experts and delegates will all have ideas about the direction of your sector, and you can also look at what companies in your sector are doing elsewhere in the world. It's one of the reasons I am so pleased that we now have spas in our hotels (and many of our clubs), as this means I absolutely have to try out the spas of rival hotel owners around the world. It's obviously very hard work, but how else am I to find out what innovations might be out there?

Implementing change

In business, change brings opportunity, and those companies that respond to change in a way that meets their customers' needs will be the ones that increase their turnover. Anticipating and responding to changing needs is how smaller companies become bigger companies. Identifying change isn't enough though: it needs to be methodically implemented.

When you change anything in a business, it's never as simple as 'buy new computer, use new computer'. You will need to tell your staff and your customers about the change, you may need to train them to use the new technology, and there may be several glitches as you all get used to the new equipment. It's completely understandable why some companies – and company managers – are reluctant to embrace change. But those are the very same companies that will see their profits slowly but surely begin to slide.

QUESTION

What's my profit?

THIS HAS GOT TO BE THE MOST IMPORTANT QUESTION that anyone in business can ask themselves. Your business might have many aims – to provide local employment, to raise money for good causes, to make your customers' lives better – but unless you turn a profit, you won't be able to do anything else. Put simply, the fundamental reason a business exists is to produce a profit. So how big is yours?

Vanity v sanity

One of my favourite phrases in business is that 'turnover is vanity, and profit is sanity'. Whenever an entrepreneur or CEO talks to me about his or her turnover, it's usually because they're too embarrassed to talk about their profit. Or, occasionally, it's because they don't actually know the difference between the two. So forgive me if I spell out the most basic business lesson you've ever received: turnover is all the money that your business generates, or the total value of all your sales; and profit is everything you have left after you have paid all your bills.

It is entirely possible for a company to have a multi-million-pound turnover and fail to make a profit. Look at Woolworths. While you can't make a profit without first producing some turnover, at the end of the day, it's really only the profit that matters. I would rather have a company with a £5m turnover and a £2m profit than a £500m turnover and a £1m profit.

Over the years, I've lost count of the number of entrepreneurs who have told me that their business makes a '£50k profit' or even a '£2m profit' and then, when I ask how much they earn, tell me that their profit is their income. Let me be really, really clear about this: your profit is what's left *after* you've paid all your bills *and* paid yourself.

Calculating profit

The standard term for calculating your profit is annually. This is because retailers will do well in the run-up to Christmas, holiday companies will do well in the summer, restaurants do well on Mother's Day and florists coin it in on Valentine's Day. Unless you've been in business for less than a year, annual profit is the important number you need to know.

The biggest problem inexperienced business owners encounter when they calculate their profit is that they fail to include all their costs. Leaving out their own salary is the most common mistake, but omitting casual expenses or overheads is frequently done, especially when they're running family businesses where the line between what's a business expense and what's a family one is easily crossed.

The other mistake I see most often is confusion between pre- and post-tax profits. If you've ever seen an accountant's ledger, then you'll be familiar with the term PBIT – profit before interest and tax. This is the figure that potential buyers or investors would use to determine the value of your company, and it is often a figure that flatters. The reason for this is that if your company was bought by an offshore company for cash, then they could keep all your PBIT for themselves. However, if your company has any outstanding loans, or is liable for tax, then the amount you will be left with after your bank and the Inland Revenue have taken their slice will be significantly less. To give you a rough idea of the difference between PBIT and actual profit, a couple of years ago, Bannatyne Fitness's PBIT was around £18m, but after we made our loan interest payments and handed over several million in corporation tax, the company was left with around £7m. That's a pretty substantial difference.

There is another way that creative accountancy can inflate your profits, and that's by including company assets on your profit and loss accounts. Let's just say that a high-street shop has a trading loss for the year of £80,000, but the business has £100,000 of stock, then that stock is added to the ledger to show a £20k profit. But as it's money you can't spend, it's not really a profit, is it?

Advice for employees

It's not just employers and business owners that should be calculating profit: I would encourage employees to have a go at estimating their boss's profit, because it is very valuable information. Let's say that you work in a high-street shop and you are paid £20k a year, and that three people work in the shop with you. You can instantly calculate that the shop owner's salary bill is £80k, and when you add on things like holiday pay and employer's NI contributions, it will probably be over £100k. By looking at commercial letting agents' websites, you could probably make a good estimate of what your boss pays for rent, rates and utilities. If you see the orders and sign for deliveries, you can probably work out how much your boss pays your suppliers. And if you cash up at the end of the day, you should have a very good idea of what the shop's weekly turnover is. You now have all the information you need to tot up how much profit your boss is making.

The bigger the company, the harder it will be to do this, but it's possible for many employees to make a good estimate of the value of their company's contracts and to subtract the likely costs. Then all you have to do is ask yourself one simple question: does this add up?

You might think that your boss is coining it in and making money hand over fist. If that's the case, then you probably want to find ways to impress your boss, secure a promotion and argue for a pay rise. But if you think the sums simply don't add up, then you might want to start thinking about what else you should be doing. A business that doesn't turn a profit won't be in business for very long.

QUESTION

What's my most profitable line?

I'VE ALREADY TALKED ABOUT IDENTIFYING YOUR BEST-selling line, but it's not necessarily the case that your bestseller will also be the most profitable thing you sell. The Great British pub offers one of the best examples of how bestsellers and big profits aren't always the same thing. I'd be willing to bet that the item every pub in the country sells the most of is beer, but the profit margin on each pint could probably be less than 40 per cent. If a beer is heavily promoted, the margin might be as low as 10 or 20 per cent. The average profit on a bottle of wine, however, is usually a lot higher: a bottle bought for £3 can retail at £14, giving a profit margin of 78 per cent, or more if sold by the glass. But the items a pub makes the most profit on aren't even alcoholic: soft drinks (especially those from a pump dispenser) can offer mark-ups of several hundred per cent on their cost price. You should never feel embarrassed about buying a round of soft drinks: your bartender will be only too happy to serve you.

Identifying your most profitable line can help your business in a number of ways. For starters, simply by going through this analysis you will understand your business so much better, but you will also gain all sorts of insights that can be applied to the rest of your organisation. If you can work out why one product produces more profit than another, you can use that information to make a bigger margin on the rest of your offering.

At first glance, it seems really easy to calculate your profit on each of your lines, especially if you're in the business of selling merchandise: you simply deduct your cost price from your sales price, right? Unfortunately, it's not quite so simple: there are all sorts of other costs – like storage, training, transport, staffing and wastage – that mean high-margin goods aren't always high-profit.

Perhaps it's easier to explain if I go back to the pub example. Let's say that the single item with the biggest margin that the pub sells is a premium vodka brand. If a bottle has a wholesale cost of £15, and a landlord can get 40 measures from the bottle and sell them at £3 each, that makes a turnover of £120. It's a very nice mark-up, but only if those are the only costs involved. There might be all sorts of hidden costs like:

- Specialist refrigeration – punters expect their premium vodkas to be ice-cold.

- Staff training – you're never going to sell the premium brand unless your staff have been trained to sell the higher-priced brand to customers.

- Staff time – premium drinks tend to be 'dressed' with accessories like citrus twists that take time to prepare, time that could be spent serving other customers.

- Wastage – there will always be a small amount that gets spilled or left in the bottle. In the case of wine, if a bottle has been open for any length of time, any unsold product will have to be tipped down the sink.

You get the picture. A pub might actually make more profit from a mainstream brand than a premium brand. It's the same for lots of other businesses: their high profile products aren't necessarily their profit drivers. And for other businesses, like the airline industry, it's the opposite: some airlines make most of their profits from less than 10 per cent of their customers – those who travel in business and first class. The cost of offering them priority check-in, private waiting lounges and more space and choice onboard is not that much higher than the cost of carrying an economy-class passenger, which is why airlines are much more interested in attracting business and first-class travellers. If you can work out which products or services you make the most profit from, then you will also know which of your customers and clients deserve more of your attention.

If you go through every product and service your business sells and itemise the costs for each of them – including putting a price on things like man hours, or storage – then you will start to see if there are some lines you should be pushing harder, and some that aren't worth the bother. If you can buy a product for £10 and sell it for £100, it might not actually be worth it if it requires £50 of staff time and £40 to store and maintain it.

This rigorous analysis of your business, or your department, gives you the information and ammunition you need to ditch the areas of your business that drag you down and hold you back. And, of course, if you do that, while simultaneously pushing to sell more of your high-margin goods, it also allows you to start making a lot more money!

Is it investible?

IF ONLY EVERYONE WHO CAME INTO *DRAGONS' DEN* GAVE this question some thought! People often assume that if a good business comes into the Den then one of us will inevitably put our money in. The truth is that there are lots of good businesses that fail to get our backing, and there are a handful of very good reasons why: either the entrepreneur is asking for too much money for too little equity, the business is in a field that none of us is interested in getting into, or we just might not like the person presenting enough to spend more time with them! But the most common reason why a good business doesn't get investment is because it isn't actually investible.

Too many people have come into the Den thinking that the pitch they should make to the Dragons is the same as the pitch they might make to a bank manager. A bank is looking for two things that we're not interested in: a) evidence that you will be able to meet your repayments on a loan, and b) assets that exceed the value of the loan that can be seized if you fail to make your repayments.

An investor, on the other hand, puts money into a business for one single, solitary reason: to make more money. If they can't get a decent return on their money within a reasonable time period, then you're going to find it very hard to persuade them that it's worth the risk. If you run a business that is looking for investment, either from a Dragon, an angel, or a venture capitalist, then it will help you to see your business from an investor's point of view. If you can't give us at least a 25 per cent return on our capital in a two- to three-year time frame, forget it. For many investors that simply isn't enough of a return to justify the risk: unless you are projecting a 100 per cent return, you'll not get their backing.

These are the reasons why a really sound business might also be an uninvestible business:

1. It's too small

If an entrepreneur is looking for a £20k investment, it doesn't really matter if they are projecting a 100 per cent return, because most investors will think that it's just not worth their time. Their energies – and money – would be better placed on a new business that has the chance to grow into a really big business. It's not that we don't value the £20k we stand to make; it's that we'll make a lot more than £20k if we invest in a bigger project. By and large, small businesses don't interest professional investors.

2. It's too soon

You'll be familiar with the phrase 'no risk, no reward', and the main skill of a successful investor is to assess the risks and rewards on offer. The more we are able to weigh the risks, the more willing we are to share in the potential rewards. One of the best ways we assess the risks is by looking at a business's past – its orders, its profits, its growth. If there's no track record to look at, we can't make a judgement. What it comes down to – as regular viewers of *Dragons' Den* will know – is that many people are coming to us with little more than an idea. The only way you can invest in an idea is if you own a very large slice of it, and that is almost always unpalatable to the person who had the idea in the first place.

3. It's too complicated

If you want an investor to put money into your patented widget, it really helps if that widget, the patent, the prototypes and the business are owned by the same company. It also helps if the widget company doesn't own lots of other gizmos that the investor is not interested in. Often *Den* participants have come to us offering a slice of an invention but not the business, or a percentage of the company but not the revenue, or a piece of a subsidiary but not the holding company. If the structure of ownership and operation of your business is not completely transparent, then you make it very hard for an investor not to think that you're hiding something. It might all be perfectly legal and thought through, but it makes you look shady, and it also makes it much harder to assess the opportunity.

4. There's no exit strategy

And now for another familiar phrase: a return on investment. Note the word 'return'. It's incredible to me just how many people don't realise that at some point an investor is going to want to get their money back. An investor doesn't just want to know how your business is going to make them money, they need to know when and how they will get their money (and any profit) back. We do not want to put money into a business so that you can run it for a nice little profit for the rest of your career: we want the biggest possible return in the shortest possible time frame. Traditionally, the ways in which this happens include a stock-market flotation, where the investor's stake is converted into tradeable shares, or a trade sale to a third party who buys the investor's stake. Less common is a buy-back arrangement where the business founder uses profits to buy back the investor's stake.

If you come to the conclusion that your business is not investible, then you need to look around for alternative sources of funding. The most common source is a bank loan, and while the repayments may cause some short-term pain, in the long term you still own 100 per cent of your business. You might also get funding from grants (from time to time, some councils, charities and the government all make grants available to businesses that help them meet their aims).

If none of these are an option, then you have to write your business plan to take account of this. It is perfectly possible to grow businesses more slowly without the booster fuel of investment, so long as you steadily plough some of your profits back into your business.

The important thing to remember is that if you try to seek investment for a business that ultimately is not investible, you haven't just wasted the time of the investors you've approached, you've wasted your own time. And all the energy you put into projections and presentations could have gone into growing your business in a less flashy but ultimately more sensible way.

The thing that is always forgotten about investibility is that it isn't just something for business owners to think about: employees should too. Obviously, as an employee, you're unlikely to know details about ownership structures and equity stakes, but you might know enough about the company to make good guesses about the potential of the business. Given what you know about the company, and given what you know about investors' thirst for profits, ask yourself if you think your employer is investible. If you do, then fantastic: you are working for a company that is going places. If you don't, it's by no means a disaster, but it's the kind of information you can factor into future career choices. If you're ambitious, you should want to work for the kind of business that can give its employees a return on their investment of time and energy in the same way investors look for a return on capital.

QUESTION

What should next year's profit be?

WHETHER YOU RUN YOUR OWN BUSINESS OR A DIVISION of someone else's, your answer to this question will help you see the future a little more clearly. Targets are really important in business, as they give you focus and keep you motivated. The power of working out what next year's profit should be is that you'll be more likely to reach your targets.

I've already said that, ultimately, the main reason for a business to exist is to make money. No profit = no business, but that doesn't necessarily mean that the bigger your profit is, the healthier your business becomes. If you grow your business too fast, or spend your profits rather than invest them, you could be jeopardising long-term stability. So this chapter is about working out what is the right course to set for your business in the year ahead.

Go for growth?

The first aspect you need to consider is whether or not your business can grow in the coming year. I wish I could say that a good business leader can always grow their business, but the truth is that there are times when even very experienced leaders or well-established businesses will struggle. Many businesses and industries are cyclical, and the amount of growth you can achieve will depend on where you are in that cycle. At the beginning of a boom, it is relatively easy to grow a business, but in the current economic climate, Bannatyne Fitness won't be the only company that will find growth difficult. While our members cut back their expenditure and banks tighten their lending criteria, consolidation will be our aim.

Other businesses in other industries will continue to have opportunities to grow, however. It's said that pawn brokers, bankruptcy specialists and manufacturers of anti-depressants do well in a downturn, but there will be many other kinds of businesses that will find opportunities in the years ahead. Large multinationals will look for growth by exploiting markets in the emerging economies of Asia and South America. Innovative start-ups would hope to see a rapid expansion of their business and their profits in the early years (after all, if a start-up doesn't grow, it'll go bust). Some businesses will look to capitalise if their rivals go to the wall. So even when the economy falters, there are chances for businesses to grow their profits. However, there will also be businesses operating in industries in decline – like magazine and newspaper publishing, or high-street booksellers – who know their best years are behind them.

When you take into account the industry you're in, the

cycle of the economy and how well-established your business is, you should be able to come to a conclusion about whether your targets for growth (and therefore profits) should tend towards ambitious or achievable.

The power of ambition

Talking of ambition, you shouldn't underestimate its power to make things happen. I realise I risk sounding like one of those hyper motivational speakers, but sometimes having the ambition to achieve is actually the foundation of achievement. An ambitious target can create the pressure and dynamism that gets results, even in tough economic times

The title of this chapter is 'What *should* next year's profit be?' As someone in charge of a business, or a large part of a business, you will have some control over the direction the company takes, which means you have some influence on how much money your company will make in the next year. If you give your team an ambitious target, if you motivate and reward them properly, there is a chance that simply by saying you are going to achieve profits of £XXm, you end up working harder to make the money.

I think it's possible to downgrade forecasts too much when there are strong economic headwinds, and those businesses who lack ambition risk suffering more than they need to. It's still possible for businesses to operate with greater efficiency, to explore new markets and bring out new products. When setting your targets for the coming year, a little ambition could add quite a lot to your bottom line.

A realistic target

After 30-odd years in business, I've come to the conclusion that looking for an average of 20 per cent growth in profits each year is about right. On profits of £10k a year, that works out at only another £2k, and on profits of £1m, finding an additional £200k should be plausible. If you look to increase your profits by more than 20 per cent, you increase the risk of encountering cash-flow problems and lending difficulties, or creating internal difficulties because of inadequate management structures. If you look for less than 20 per cent, then you're not hungry enough and could be vulnerable to a challenge from a more dynamic rival.

The 20 per cent target should be adjusted to take account of the issues I've outlined above: some years you'll aim for slightly more, some years you'll have to settle for slightly less. But if you take your company's growth over a longer period, perhaps a decade, then an average of 20 per cent is a meaningful benchmark to aim for. The key here – no matter what the prevailing economic conditions – is that you set a target, whether it's optimistic or pessimistic, as that target allows you to plan ahead and allocate resources more efficiently.

QUESTION 10

Who's my best client?

IN THE NINTH SERIES OF *DRAGONS' DEN*, A YOUNG entrepreneur came in to ask for investment. He worked for the family business, which had made its money for a couple of generations by manufacturing shoes. As part of our examination of his business, we asked him about the company's trading history, and for three years in a row it had made a loss. 'How can this company have stayed afloat if you keep making losses?' we asked. His answer highlights how difficult it is to say who your best client is. 'Well,' he said, 'we used to get 60 per cent of our business from Woolworths. We are now in the process of rebuilding the company since they went bust.' It doesn't seem unreasonable to think that the client that is responsible for 60 per cent of your business is your best client, but actually they could just as easily be your bogeyman.

The ideas and suggestions in this chapter are designed to help you think about how important individual clients are to your business, and whether you need to be doing more to hold on to them. Let's start with something simple: money.

Your most lucrative client

Have you ever broken down your income according to which company or client that revenue came from? It's a really simple exercise that can reveal which clients you should be taking greater care of. An agency with ten clients will find it pretty easy to work out who their most lucrative client is, but if you have hundreds of thousands of clients, it might be more helpful to talk about *types* of clients rather than individual people or companies. In my hotel business, a good proportion of our visitors are corporate travellers, while much of our weekend business comes from wedding parties. It helps me to plan the expansion of the hotel business to distinguish between the different types of guest – business, wedding, honeymoon, spa break etc.

Whether you have five clients or 500,000 customers, if you can identify the traits and characteristics of your most lucrative client, then you can start to look for those traits in other people and target them to become future clients. Digging down into your accounts will give you the information you need to steer the business in a more profitable direction.

Your most cost-effective client

Let's imagine an advertising agency with ten clients who pay fees ranging from £750,000 a year (Client A) to £150,000 (Client B). The agency spends 1,500 hours a year on Client A and 250 hours on Client B. Client A brings in revenue of £500 an hour, and Client B £600. Client A might bring in more *turnover*, but if we assume that the agency's hourly costs are constant, the more contracts they can win from clients like Client B, the more *profit* they will make. It doesn't actually matter how much revenue a client brings in if you don't make a profit from the contract (although there are rare exceptions, as we'll see in a moment).

The great thing about doing this kind of analysis is that not only do you discover who your most cost-effective client is, you also find out who your least cost-effective client is. If you can work out why one particular client, or one particular *type* of client, takes up more of your time or resources, then you can either a) try to avoid working with those clients again, b) avoid doing that kind of work again, or c) renegotiate more favourable terms when you next start a contract.

Your most influential client

There are some circumstances in which a company would take on a contract that doesn't make them much money, and one of them is when a client is influential. If a client can bring in other clients, or has so much prestige that other people will want to hire you because you've worked with someone so well respected, then they might be worth doing business with, even if there's no profit in it. Sometimes landing a contract with the right client can transform the fortunes of a business, especially if that client then becomes an advocate for your company and starts to open doors for you.

Sometimes, however, a client can have undue influence over a company. If, for example, you spend much of your time devoted to one client at the expense of others, then you risk losing the other clients' custom. If you align your business closely with one client and something happens to your relationship with that client, then you may struggle to survive the termination of that contract, just like the shoe manufacturer who came into the Den.

Keeping your most valuable client

By now you should have a reasonable idea of who your most profitable and influential clients are. The next question you need to ask yourself is: what would happen if they stopped being your client? What would that mean for your turnover, your profits, your staff and your status within the industry? If there's any risk at all that you are too reliant on your client's patronage, then you must look at ways of preventing the worst from happening.

There are, broadly, two ways to do this: the first is to make sure you deliver such exceptional service to your most valuable clients that they would never use one of your rivals; and the second is to make sure you do everything you can to bring in another client whose business would keep you afloat if they did terminate your contract. You should make it your business to get to know your clients' needs and businesses almost as well as you know your own. That way you can start to anticipate their needs and offer them personalised services they would find it impossible to get from a new partner, thus securing their business in the years to come.

And finally . . .

If this research has revealed that your business is lugging around some clients that don't pay very well, or that eat up your resources, or take up too much of your time, then you already know what I'm going to say: ditch 'em, and put your effort into finding clients that can help your business flourish.

Whether you run a corner shop or an international conglomerate, you can let your clients guide you towards a more profitable future if you find ways to concentrate your efforts on the clients who bring your business the greatest rewards.

QUESTION 11

Who's my next client?

THIS QUESTION COULD JUST AS EASILY BE 'WHAT'S MY next contract?' or 'Which group of customers do I target next?' It's all about looking a few weeks or months into the future and working out what your next step will be. In my experience, business owners find it very easy to imagine how successful they'll be in ten years' time, but struggle to know how they will pay the bills in a few months' time. The suggestions in this chapter will help you to plot an immediate route forward that will ultimately lead to a successful future.

Get introductions

If your customers are happy with your service, they might be happy to introduce you and recommend you to their friends. One of the best ways of getting them to do this is to incentivise them, either by giving them free gifts, or by offering a discount on their next purchase. The great thing about recruiting clients in this way is that there's no wastage, as you only pay for the clients you get.

It's almost always true that it is cheaper, easier and quicker to find future customers in the same place you found your existing ones. However, it's not always good for business for all your customers to be alike. Let's imagine an accountant who looks after the books of lots of local retailers: during a recession, the chances are that her accountancy business will suffer every bit as much as the retailers'. We're quite familiar with the idea of diversifying risk in stocks and shares portfolios, but too many people fail to apply this idea to their business.

Look for the gaps

A few years ago, I asked my team to analyse the occupancy of our health clubs throughout the day. I wasn't surprised to find out that we were at our busiest early in the morning, during lunchtime and between 5 p.m. and 7 p.m., when our members finished work. Having these figures enabled us to get our staffing levels right during the peak periods, but they also revealed something else: there were big chunks of the day when several of our clubs were practically empty. We had the staff in, the lights on and were incurring all sorts of other overheads, but had precious little income. We had found a gap; now we needed to create a market in the gap.

We realised that we didn't need many more peak member-ships, as our classes and equipment were being used to capacity at certain times of the day. The best way to grow the business was to get people to come to us when we were relatively empty. We asked ourselves a very simple question: who's around to visit a health club during the day? And we came up with a really simple answer: retired people. And so we launched our Young at Heart memberships that offer discounts for the over 55s at certain times of the day. It has been a huge success for our company, and I would recommend that anyone looking to expand their business looks for the gaps in their own company, and then comes up with a product or service to exploit the opportunity.

Identify the long-term trends

If you work in fashion or interior design, you'll be very aware of the impact of trends on your business. However *every* business and *every* industry is equally affected by fashion; it's just that some people don't realise it. The more you make yourself aware of the trends influencing your industry, the better you will be at finding, and retaining, customers.

Let me give you a very basic example. Let's say you run a plumbing company and most of your work is installing central heating in new-build houses. If the property market slumps, the long-term trend will be that fewer houses get built, which in turn means you'll get fewer contracts. If the long-term trend is that the house-building sector is in trouble, your next client should be a building maintenance company, or a construction company with contracts to build schools or hospitals in the public sector.

Who would you *like* it to be?

Another way to work out who your next client will be is to simply ask yourself who you'd like it to be. If you see your rivals landing contracts with high-profile companies, or getting work in an interesting new field, then why shouldn't you? If you think your business is ready to move up a gear, perhaps you should start targeting potential clients who will help you make the shift.

Of course, the flipside of identifying your ideal client is working out who you *don't* want it to be. If you can identify that a particular kind of customer is harder to deal with or less lucrative than another, you should use this information to turn down work that will keep you in your current position. It can be very difficult to turn down an offer of work, but if you know that dealing with a bad client stops you from tracking down and courting a better client, then you'll be prepared to take the short-term hit on your income.

Get a name and number

If you've ever been in sales and had to cold-call a potential customer, you will know how much easier it is to start a meaningful conversation with 'Can I speak to Mrs Smith, please?' rather than 'Can I speak to the householder, please?' If you are going to successfully win a new client, you need to make the right kind of introductions. And that requires research.

It's not enough for a plumber to say he needs a new maintenance client; he needs to identify the firms in his area that do that work, and then he needs to find out the name of the person who employs subcontractors. Unless you make your quest to find a new client specific, then you are going to find it hard to win their business. You'll need a name, an email address, a phone number and probably their PA's name. Maybe you should also be following potential clients on social networking sites, or making their acquaintance at industry events. The more you can make someone believe that you know and understand their requirements, the more likely it is that they'll become your next client.

QUESTION

What else should my business be doing?

IF YOUR CAREER IS GOING WELL, IF YOUR COMPANY IS making a tidy profit, then it's very easy to carry on as you are. Business as usual. It's my opinion that as soon as you start to settle, as soon as you think you've got enough, you become lazy and you start to lose ground to your rivals. You also find yourself on a bit of hamster wheel, doing the same thing day in day out and becoming bored. By asking yourself what else you should be doing, you stay alert to opportunity and keep yourself motivated.

When you're so tied up with the day-to-day of running your business, it can be hard to know where to start, so I've come up with a handful of suggestions about ways in which you can keep your business on its toes.

1. Maximise revenue streams

This is pretty standard advice, but every departmental manager and every business owner should regularly set aside time to explore whether there are any additional income streams they are missing out on. A garage, for example, might think about offering a valet service as well as crash repairs, or charging for the collection and delivery of vehicles. Or they could think about joining the Green Flag network to get additional business. Whatever your core business is, it's highly likely that there will be some add-ons and extras you can offer to your existing customers. These might not transform your business, but they often produce a decent return for relatively little effort. At Bannatyne Fitness, for example, we make additional income from serving food and selling fitness accessories. The income doesn't radically alter our profitability, but it brings in roughly an extra £500,000 in revenue a year. Since we started opening spas in some of our clubs, we now also earn additional revenue from beauty treatments and massages.

2. What are other people doing?

Another way to uncover the things you should be doing is to look at what other businesses and individuals are up to. If a colleague at the next desk is asked for their opinion more than you, or gets promoted, try to work out why they've been favoured. They might be writing an influential blog, or putting in overtime, or have overseas experience. Whatever it is, if you can replicate the behaviour of more successful people or companies, then you increase the chances that you'll also replicate their success. I have a very clear memory of seeing

Alan Sugar being interviewed on TV about his opinions on the economy, and I thought to myself: why am I not being asked for my views? What's he got that I haven't? And so I hired a PR agency and started getting involved in a few low-key documentaries, and that led to *Dragons' Den*, and now you can't get me off the telly! The point is: if someone else is doing something you want to do, don't be disheartened – be inspired.

3. What are my ambitions?

It's very easy for our jobs to take over our lives when we enjoy what we do. We can become so focused on building our businesses that we forget there might be other things we want to do with our lives and our careers. So stop for a moment and try to remember the ambitions you had when you were younger. If you find out you've been neglecting a dream or ambition, you might regret not doing anything about it if you leave it until it's too late. Often, connecting with child-hood dreams can be a powerful motivation to get on and do the thing that got shoved to one side when you started your career.

4. Where's the problem?

Another way of finding out where you, or your business, should dedicate some time and effort is to look at where you have problems. If one part of your business is causing difficulties, or if one member of your team is the source of friction, or if your customers keep complaining about the same thing, there's a pretty good chance that something has been overlooked. Identifying the pain, the problems and the pinch points can help you target your energies – and very often small changes can make a big difference.

What do my customers want next?

Working out what your customers want before they know they want it is the best way of growing and strengthening your business. If you can identify the trends in your industry, or the products that are getting attention at trade fairs, then it becomes obvious what you should be doing.

Whether you're the kind of boss who formally reviews your company's performance at annual intervals, or someone who does their best thinking in taxis, these are the sorts of questions that can help you grow your business and prevent stagnation. Continually asking the 'what else' question means that you always stay one step ahead of your customers – *and* the competition.

QUESTION

Who's not pulling their weight?

HAVING SOMEONE ON YOUR TEAM WHO DOESN'T PULL
their weight a) costs you money, b) prevents your company
from maximising its potential, and c) demoralises the people
who work around them. Whether you run several departments
or teams, or just one, if you can identify your slackers, you can
improve more than just morale – productivity, profits and
performance will also start to shoot up.

As chairman of Bannatyne Fitness, I am no longer involved
in the day-to-day running of our health clubs. My chief
executive runs the company, and he delegates to regional
managers who support and motivate our club managers who
in turn look after the staff in each individual club. I haven't
met everyone we employ, and as I trust my managers to run
their departments as they see fit, you might think that I can't
possibly know who's not pulling their weight. You'd be wrong:

I might not know individual employees' names, but I scrutinise our company data to see which club and which services aren't measuring up. If I see that a club or a region isn't performing as well as others, then I will start looking for reasons why.

Not all managers and business owners will have access to the kind of data that Bannatyne Fitness produces. If you don't collect this kind of data, then your first step should be to put in place new data collection procedures. The following are some of the areas you should look to quantify.

Measure productivity

This is a very crude tool for measuring the contribution of your staff, but along with all the other suggestions that follow, it helps you to build up a picture of what's really going on inside your organisation.

If you are a manufacturer, you could calculate how many units each worker produces in a week, a month or a year. Or you could break it down into an hourly figure. If you are a magazine publisher, you could see how many articles each of your journalists writes per issue, or how many pages they fill, or perhaps even how many words they write. Whatever your industry, there will be a measurable unit you can break output down into. You could then cross-reference this information with each worker's salary and work out how much each unit costs you.

I hope my last example exposes just how crude a measure this is, because a journalist's major contribution may not be how many words they write, but how good or influential those words are, or the subject those words are written about is. A productivity measure misses out on all those value judgements that let a manager assess the worth of individual team members. Nor does it recognise that some of your workers may have other responsibilities that reduce their hours at the coalface, or recognise the contribution they make in other ways (like gelling the team together or contributing ideas). For that reason, you also need to measure other aspects of your workforce, like . . .

Time-keeping

Do you know the easiest way to wind up your colleagues? It's by not putting in the same hours as they do. No one likes to work with a slacker, so if there's someone on your team who always comes in late, takes long lunch breaks and slips out early, then you have someone in your midst who is breeding resentment. Just like the productivity measure, time-keeping on its own can't tell you if someone isn't pulling their weight (after all, the reason some people get in early and leave late is because they spend all day gossiping or on Facebook), but cross-referenced with the productivity data, this can help you build up an idea of which workers, or departments, or in my case health clubs, produce the greatest output per hour worked.

Keeping records of time-keeping can be problematic, unless you have a swipe-card system for all staff that automatically logs when people arrive and leave. However, it's standard practice that – for health and safety reasons – the building owner or manager should know precisely how many people are on the premises in case an evacuation is necessary. Which means most offices will have a daily log of who is in the building. It doesn't take too much effort to extend the taking of this kind of daily register to include 'time in' and 'time out'. Another way to measure the hours someone puts in is by asking your IT team to record the times your server was accessed by individual computer users.

Task-setting

Another simple way of seeing which members of your team are performing below par is to set each of them the same task and see who carries it out the fastest, or to the highest standard. Again, it's a pretty brutal way to assess your team, but it might illuminate a problem.

If you start to think that there is a team member who is affecting everyone else's performance, you can always experiment with your team structure. If you are able to get a potential troublemaker to work on another project for a while, you can see if the team does better when they are out of the picture. Alternatively, see if there is a pattern between your productivity measures and the times when different workers are on holiday.

Gut instinct

The truth is that you probably already know who isn't pulling their weight. If you're any good at leading your team, then you've probably observed confrontations or heard gossip that someone isn't putting in the same hours, the same commitment or the same effort as everyone else. Current employment law makes it very difficult to remove employees who don't perform at the required level, and this I think means that managers assume there's not much they can do about it. In fact, it's entirely probable that you've known for years who your weak performers are; you've just avoided doing something about it.

The good news is that the data you've collected on productivity and time-keeping will give you the proof of underperformance that will help you confront the glaringly obvious: something needs to be done. But before you take action, you need to confront something just as awkward: you need to find out why an employee is underperforming.

There may be personal reasons: perhaps they have too many commitments at home, or are struggling with ill health. However, the chances are that their underperformance has more to do with something you've done – or not done – than anything in their private life. If you haven't provided them with enough training, or ensured effective oversight, or you haven't properly communicated their targets or what you expect from them, then it's no wonder that they aren't performing to their best.

Of course, there's one other thing you should consider before you take any action, and that's the possibility that the weakest link might in fact be you. Have a look at other managers, or other business owners, and see if they are getting more from their teams than you do. Is there something you can learn from them? Before you start making some of the changes I'm about to suggest, you should have a very good look in the mirror and assess your own productivity, time-keeping and effectiveness.

Now what?

If it turns out that you have a problem employee, then you need to take action. The longer you leave that person in place, the longer they have to demoralise their colleagues and reduce everyone else's productivity. Assuming that employment law will make it difficult and expensive to let them go, what are your options?

Performance-based pay

Think about moving to a system where remuneration is based on output. It's very effective at motivating your team to think about their productivity. When I ran a chain of care homes, I paid a bonus to all staff if our occupancy rates were above 98 per cent. Most of the time, I happily paid the bonus because everyone was very motivated to make sure the homes were full. The great thing about this system is that team members do a lot of the oversight for you: if they think they will miss out on their bonus because someone is slacking, you can be pretty sure the slacker will quickly get the message.

Improve training

If you invest in your staff training and ensure they have the skills to deliver at the necessary level, the chances are that overall performance will improve dramatically. If you simultaneously improve your oversight of your team, you can practically guarantee improvements. But the thing that will make the biggest difference is if you improve your communication with your team: if they know what is required of them and when, you are much more likely to get the results you require.

Redeploy

You may find that you have a brilliant worker who is under-performing simply because they are in the wrong role. If you can move someone to a position to which they are better suited, they will become an asset to your team rather than a liability.

If none of these options is viable, then you should consider starting formal disciplinary proceedings to deal with your problem employees. Occasionally, starting this process can jolt them into changing their ways, and sometimes the disciplinary process actually gives people the oversight and attention they need. Sometimes, of course, they are simply holding out for a big pay-off or a chance to sue for wrongful dismissal. So long as you abide by the regulations, if you can prove that someone is not performing and has been given adequate opportunity to train and improve, then you shouldn't be intimidated by their threats: it is possible to remove bad apples from the barrel, it just takes time. As well as a bit of money.

QUESTION

Can I survive a downturn?

I WAS ONCE GIVEN A FANTASTIC ILLUSTRATION OF WHAT a recession really means: it's like the tide is going out and you get to see who's been skinny-dipping! Recessions are really effective at revealing vulnerable assets. In good financial times, a bit of common sense will keep most businesses afloat, but in difficult times, weak and flawed businesses go under. This chapter is all about making sure you've got your swimming trunks on.

Since 2007, the world economy has been sailing in unchartered waters (I think I might stop with this nautical stuff now!) and while we haven't technically been in recession the whole time – that requires two consecutive quarters of 'negative growth', i.e. the economy shrinking – it's been a very tough climate for most businesses. If you're still in business, you might think you already know that you're recession-proof, but if the global turmoil has taught us any-thing, it's that none of us can predict the future. Even if you're entirely confident in your firm's prospects, you still might learn something from – or even just be reassured by – the rest of this chapter.

Only strong businesses survive recessions, and the only strength that really matters is cash. Even if you've got a strong brand, a strong marketing campaign, or some really strong products, they won't count for anything unless you also have a strong balance sheet. In a recession, cash really is king.

The first steps of business survival are pretty basic: maximise your income and minimise your costs. If you've discovered what your bestsellers are (Chapter 1), learnt all you can from your most profitable lines (Chapter 7) and cut out your deadwood (Chapter 13), then you'll have given your business the best possible chance of surviving tough con-ditions. But there's another defence you can have against going under, and that's a sensitivity analysis.

A sensitivity analysis lets you see just how robust your business is and alerts you to problems before you encounter them, which in turn gives you a chance to make interventions that can save your business. To conduct a sensitivity analysis, you just need a set of your latest accounts. Then all you do is play around with the figures.

Amend the data to see what would happen if your costs went up by 5 per cent. If your turnover dropped by 10–20 per cent, are you still in the black? What you want to find out is how far your revenue can fall and/or your costs can rise before you go into the red. The bigger the percentage change you can withstand, the more robust your business is.

I think there are three very good reasons why every

business owner should carry out regular sensitivity tests:

1. It gives you a fresh perspective

   In business, we are mostly interested in the bottom line: how much money are we actually making? For many managers, so long as that figure is big enough, they feel pretty relaxed. Being able to report to your boss or your shareholders that you made £1m in post-tax profit sounds great, but if your sensitivity analysis shows that your whopping profit is produced on a tiny margin, then your business really isn't very secure. A small percentage increase in your costs, or a decrease in your profits, could wipe out a huge slice of your earnings, or possibly even wipe the business out altogether. If you know that all that's standing between you and your millions is a 5 per cent cushion, you might behave rather differently than if you had a 50 per cent cushion.

2. It's an early warning system

   Just as a smoke alarm wakes you up in the night to give you a better chance of escaping a fire, so a sensitivity analysis can be your wake-up call to danger for your business. If you know in advance that your business will go under if revenues dip by 10–20 per cent, then you'll know you need to take action should they start to slide, whether that's cost-cutting or finding ways to increase revenue. Without a sensitivity analysis, you might only realise you're in danger when it's already too late.

3. It gives you confidence

   If you know your business can survive a 10 per cent drop in revenue, then you're not going to panic when your income drops by 5 per cent. As long as the financial reality stays within the margins you've identified, you can continue to operate with confidence.

There are a couple of features of the current financial situation that are worth including in your sensitivity analysis: inflation and interest rates. With central banks printing money and governments keen to reduce the value of their debts, we can be pretty sure that higher inflation than we've been used to will be a feature of financial life for a while. What inflation means is that even if your business stays the same, you will be worse off, because the real value of your profits will be eroded, while the real price of your costs will rise. The RPI (Retail Prices Index) has been above the government target of 2 per cent for many years, and has been as high as 5 per cent. It's worth spending some time working out what impact 5 per cent inflation for five years would have on your business.

We're also in a period of historically low interest rates. If your business is heavily geared – i.e. you have a lot of debt – you will be particularly vulnerable when rates inevitably start to rise. An increase of 1 per cent might not sound a lot, but if you owe millions of pounds, believe me, that has a massive impact on your profits.

When you do your sensitivity analysis, pay close attention to your biggest expenditures. If it's your staffing costs, for example, a 1 per cent increase in employers' NI contributions could hit you hard, whereas if it's an imported raw material, a small shift in commodity prices or exchange rates will hurt the most.

Tiny percentage shifts can have massive consequences. For example, in 2011, the VAT rate increased from 17.5 per cent to 20 per cent. That 2.5 per cent difference might not sound a lot, but on a turnover of £100m, that's an extra £2.5m you're handing over to the Revenue each year. If you're operating on small margins, something like that will cause you real pain. A sensitivity analysis gives you a chance to make adjustments before the new rates come into force.

I really can't stress enough how useful I find sensitivity analyses. I use them all the time, in all my businesses. While the economy remains fragile, they're a fantastic tool for ensuring you have enough cash in your business to get through the tough times ahead.

QUESTION

What do I waste money on?

WHENEVER I TALK ABOUT REDUCING COSTS, I RISK sounding like a caricature of a penny-pinching Scot. Maybe it's because I grew up in a house where there was absolutely no money to spare, or maybe it's because I've worked too hard for what I've got to squander it, but either way, I hate wasting money for one very good reason: it's really bad for business.

As an investor, one of the phrases I come across is 'burn rate', which is the pace at which the founders of a company I invest in will spend my money. The higher the burn rate, the less time they give their business to find its feet before the money runs out. When businesses start producing a profit, I've noticed that CEOs stop talking about their burn rate because it's assumed that income will now cover their costs. In my experience, when CEOs stop worrying about expenditure, they should start worrying about running out of cash:

no matter how big or well-established your business is, you neglect your costs at your peril.

You'll find this chapter most helpful by looking at your biggest expenditure first, and then moving on to your second biggest expenditure, and so on. For most businesses, that's usually debt repayments, rent and salaries. Because these represent such a large part of your outgoings, even if you are only able to decrease your spend by a small percentage, it can make a massive difference to your bottom line.

Debt repayments

It is entirely possible to borrow the same amount from two different lenders and pay back vastly different amounts of money. Always making sure you get the lowest possible interest rates should be second nature to business owners, but just like domestic borrowers who let their mortgages drift onto their bank's standard rate at the end of an introductory period, many CEOs let their company give too much money to the bank. Let's face it, the banks have had enough of our money in the past few years, so whatever you do, check the rates you are being charged on your debts. Then look at the rates other lenders are offering, and then see if you can switch.

Although interest rates are at historic lows (0.5 per cent at the time of writing), debt is still expensive, with banks charging way above the base rate while stinging borrowers with arrangement fees. Banks have tightened up their lending criteria, and this may mean you don't pass a new lender's thresholds, but you should still negotiate with your existing lender. If you can convince them that their punitive rates mean you risk going out of business and taking their loan with you, then you may be able to get a temporary reduction in rates.

I recently looked at the lending levels at Bannatyne Fitness and was shocked at how difficult the lending market had become. But when I offered to put all the company's debt with a single lender, the size of the loan meant they were willing to offer a very competitive rate. Perhaps you can do something similar.

Rent

I've never had a fancy office in my life, because I just don't see the point in paying for something you don't need, whether that's extra space, a prestigious address, or the 'luxury' of being in serviced buildings where you are charged over the odds for cleaning and maintenance.

One of the fortunate things that happen in a recession is that commercial rents come down (for a very unfortunate reason, of course: other businesses are going bust). With so much commercial space lying empty, there are some deals to be had: Bannatyne Fitness recently made the decision to close one of our loss-making clubs when the lease on the premises came up for renewal, but when we told the landlord of our decision, he offered us a 50 per cent reduction in rent, because he didn't think he could find another tenant. That loss-making club now produces a tidy profit. You may be able to negotiate something similar yourself.

Salaries

If you are overstaffed, then it is costing you a fortune. If you have staff who regularly take two-hour lunch breaks and still get their work done, or who spend half their day online, then you have more people in your organisation than you need. Perhaps you should be considering a recruitment freeze, or even redundancies.

That's not the only way you can waste money on salaries: if you're paying over the odds, then you are throwing money away. Let's just say you have 100 staff and pay each of them an average of £1,000 a year over the going rate: that's a huge impact on your profitability (and for many people, an extra grand a year is not going to make them any more loyal or work any harder).

Another way to reduce salary costs is to use more self-employed workers, which means you don't have additional employers' NI contributions to make. You could also look at reducing any extras you pay for, like travel or pensions. Obviously these are the kinds of changes that can infuriate workers – and their unions – but if you think your business is offering perks that aren't particularly valued by your staff, then you might be able to make a big reduction in your overheads.

As well as the big money-eaters, every business will have its own individual expenses and spending habits that might be unnecessary. It's always worth your while to sit down with your accounts and see where the money goes. Start by looking for your biggest outgoings and ask yourself if they seem reasonable. If, say, your biggest expenditure is on advertising, think about whether or not you're getting value for money from your campaigns. Or if your biggest payments go in professional fees to agents or lawyers, question whether or not you think their services are worth what you pay. I always make sure that I pay a fixed fee for services from professionals like architects and lawyers, rather than a percentage or hourly rate: it's been my experience that although paying '5 per cent of build costs' or '£100 an hour' seems good value, more often than not, you end up getting stung. If your professional fees are making your eyes water, try to negotiate a flat rate.

Unless you really scrutinise your costs, it's difficult to know where you're losing money. If your travel costs are very high, perhaps your staff are wasting money travelling to meetings separately, or at peak times, or even unnecessarily – perhaps a phone call would do instead. Whether it's IT, or entertaining, or the expenses you pay to non-executive directors on your board, asking if you could get any or all of them cheaper is the sort of thing any responsible manager should do as a matter of course.

If you're in manufacturing and your raw materials represent a big percentage of your costs, then shopping around for the most competitive suppliers makes a lot of sense. No matter what your business, it's always worth checking that you are paying the lowest possible price for all your supplies.

And remember, Bannatyne's First Rule of Business is that no one ever needs to pay for paperclips – just keep the ones from your incoming post and you'll save a fortune (well, a few pounds)!

However . . .

There are some businesses where wasting money is the only way to make money. Where would drug companies be, for example, if they didn't research and trial thousands of new drugs every year, so that just a handful will pass the tests and go on sale?

Much has been written about Google letting its boffins only work four days a week in the job they're actually employed to do, leaving them one day a week to experiment with new applications and innovations. On the face of it, this seems bonkers – they could massively improve productivity or reduce their costs if they put a stop to it. But Google is a company that will live or die by its ability to innovate. Some of its ventures – like the abandoned email service Google Wave – fall flat, while others – like Google Maps and Google Ads – ensure the business is accessed billions of times a day by millions, if not billions, of people. If Google *didn't* waste money on development, it wouldn't be nearly such a big business.

What are my company's strengths and weaknesses?

MOST SUCCESSFUL BUSINESSES REGULARLY PERFORM something called a SWOT analysis, where the senior team sits down and identifies the company's Strengths, Weaknesses, Opportunities and Threats. Some bits of corporate jargon come and go, but the SWOT analysis is still in use 50 years after it was first developed, for the simple reason that it is fantastically useful. In this chapter, I'm going to concentrate on identifying strengths and weaknesses (opportunities and threats are discussed elsewhere).

I find the best way to carry out this analysis is with a small group of people. I ask my senior team to prepare for a SWOT meeting by coming up with their own list of the company's strengths and weaknesses, because the more work you do before the meeting, the less time you will spend in the meeting. Ideally, you want someone from your accounts division to prepare comparison figures between you and your rivals, someone from your marketing department to prepare data on your brand in relation to your rivals' brands, someone from your sales force to prepare sales data, and so on.

There are a handful of characteristics on which all companies compete, and you will probably find it useful to grab a big sheet of paper (or the electronic equivalent) and use the following headings to systematically analyse your business's strengths and weaknesses against those of your rivals. Of course, you should also add categories that are specific to your industry, so what follows is just a guide, but it will hopefully give you an idea of the things you should consider.

Finances

Even if you can't get hold of your rivals' accounts, you can scrutinise your own balance sheet to see where you might be vulnerable. Are your interest rates too high? Are your profit margins too narrow? Do you have enough cash in the bank to cope with an emergency? Try to build up a picture of how financially secure your business is.

Product

How does your product stand up to other choices in the market? Get your team to assess it for its quality, branding, reliability and value for money. Be tough on your products and try to find as many faults as possible.

Service

Now ask your team for their thoughts on how your service compares with your rivals'. Do your customers feel looked after? How easily can they get their queries dealt with? How quickly do they get served? It may help to bring examples of letters of complaint you've received, or indeed letters of praise, or feedback from online forums. What are you getting right? What are your rivals getting wrong?

Value

Do you offer good value to your customers? Do you offer better value than your rivals. This isn't just about asking if you are cheaper than an alternative provider; it's about working out whether what you offer the marketplace is priced according to the benefits you deliver.

Marketing

Look at advertising campaigns your business has run recently, or add up the coverage you've had in the media: are you getting your message across? How does your marketing compare with your rivals'? Compare everything: the design of your ads, the response rate you got and the brand awareness they created.

Convenience

There's lots to consider in this section, from the methods of payment you accept to whether or not you have enough visitor parking. Look at the ways potential customers interact with your rivals, and see if there is something they are doing that you are not.

Innovation

Are you an innovator or a follower? Innovation can be a strength *and* a weakness. If you are too experimental, you can waste time and energy developing products and services no one wants. Yet if you don't respond to change, your customers will drift away.

Experience

Again, experience may not always be a strength (although it usually comes in handy). For one business, having a team that has been in the industry for decades might be seen as their biggest asset, but for a newer business, their fresh perspective and hunger for growth will be the deciding factor in their success. Are you stuck in the mud or up for anything?

Capacity

Industries and economies change. Assessing your capacity to respond to change, and your ability to capitalise on it, is key to finding out if you are vulnerable. Do you have the manpower to take on new contracts? If a new rival launched, could you cope with the competition? You might be secure in the short term, but this section is about knowing how robust you'll be in the future.

Implementation

There's not much point doing this kind of analysis unless you are prepared to make changes on the back of it. If you discover that your balance sheet is bare, or your marketing isn't getting results, then you must take action.

It's also really important that you keep reviewing your strengths and weaknesses, as they will change over time. I recommend carrying out this process at least every six months.

QUESTION 17

What's the next big thing?

IF YOU CAN ANTICIPATE WHAT THE BIG TRENDS WILL BE IN the next few years, you can position your business to take advantage. I've already talked specifically about technological shifts and the impact that they can have on companies in Chapter 5, but now I want to widen the scope of what the future will bring.

Over the years, hundreds of people and products have been hailed as 'the next big thing', from the Sinclair C5, to Justin Bieber, to the Chinese economy, to graphene, a super-light substance that is stronger than steel. Our predictions aren't always accurate, but the exercise of trying to predict the future is nevertheless always a useful tool for examining what your company might have to offer future customers.

Global trends

Let's start by looking at the broad changes that, one way or another, will probably have an effect on pretty much everyone on the planet. The impact these will have on your business will depend to a great extent on what sector you are in, but each of these changes will create an economic opportunity for some businesses – and pose a threat to others. These are the kinds of trends I'm talking about:

- an ageing population

- the rise in living standards in China and India

- the impact of austerity measures put in place by Western governments

- low/high interest rates

- high/low inflation

- a generation locked out of the housing market and living with their parents

- increased energy/fuel costs

- the Arab spring

- the Occupy movement

- flexible working

- home-working

There are also technological trends to consider, like:

- the growth of mobile phone use in the developing world
- increase in broadband speeds
- increase in wifi access in public places
- improvements in computing/processing power
- social media
- the rise of apps
- cloud computing

It won't take you long to think up ten or twenty global trends of your own. The question you then need to ask yourself about each of them is: what do they mean for my business? It might not immediately be apparent how and why some of these big global trends will have an impact on your business, especially if your business isn't an international conglomerate. It's nevertheless really worth staring into your crystal ball and forcing yourself to come up with reasons – however outlandish or tangential – why these trends might affect what you do in the years to come. Sometimes, by coming up with over-the-top reactions to such trends, you accidentally stumble across the more likely ways in which your business will need to respond.

Local trends

What's going on in your territory that might change the way things are? Is there a new enterprise zone being created, or a housing estate being built? What can events in the news tell you about the things your customers are worried or excited about?

As well as watching the news and reading papers to find out what's going on, you can also get useful information from organisations like the British Chambers of Commerce, the CBI, political think tanks, polling organisations, government departments and local councils. If, for example, the government starts giving incentives for hiring younger workers, how can you benefit? Or if a motorway extension is being built near your HQ, what does that mean for your logistics and fuel costs? Might the government increase VAT, or corporation tax, or NI contributions? All these things will have an impact on your business.

One of the big lessons I learnt during my career is that where there is change, there is opportunity. I started my care home business in the 1980s, in response to changes in government legislation about the way care home fees were paid. It might be that there are currently financial incentives from national or local authorities that could transform your business.

Industrywide trends

In banking, risk assessment is increasingly computerised. In publishing, bookshops are closing. In house-building, room sizes are getting smaller. In media, everything is being personalised. In manufacturing, a weak pound is easing some of the pressure, but increasing the cost of raw materials. Whatever industry you're in, there will be trends that will have an influence over the future of your business. You should always strive to keep on top of your industry's news, by doing things like subscribing to trade publications, attending industry events, or joining trade organisations.

The interesting thing about trends is that there will always be businesses that buck the industrywide trends, whether it's a bank that offers personalised service, a bookshop that sells specially selected and recommended books, or an online newspaper that offers edited choice rather than endless articles. When you analyse the trends in your industry, it won't automatically be the case that you will make more money if you follow them: sometimes you can make faster progress on a less congested road.

Google, MySpace, Facebook, Twitter etc.

Every few years, a company becomes so influential that they create their own trends. Some, like Friends Reunited and MySpace, stop being relevant, but others potentially impact on every business on the planet. The question is, what will be the impact on yours? If, for example, you don't have a presence on Facebook, will you lose out to companies that do? Or, if Google makes the content of millions of books searchable, what will that mean for your research department? When companies have such spectacular reach into the lives of your customers and clients, it's worth considering what they will do next.

Some entrepreneurs have built hugely successful businesses on the coattails of these monster companies, like the manufacturers of iPhone covers and accessories, developers like Zynga that create games specifically for Facebook, or Tweetdeck, a website that made Twitter easier to use (and was so good that it was bought by Twitter in 2011 for £25m).

Of course, the real opportunity is working out what the next Twitter or Facebook will be. In my experience, the best way to do that is to talk to some teenagers and see what's getting their attention!

QUESTION

What might stand in my way?

THE SOONER YOU CAN ANTICIPATE PROBLEMS, THE EASIER it is to stop them causing damage to your business. By working out which companies, trends and people are likely to prevent you from achieving your goals, you can take action that will limit, or maybe even eliminate, their impact. Below are a few of the main obstacles businesses frequently stumble over.

Rivals

Imagine for a moment that you plan to open a florist. You've found a town where there isn't another florist. You've done your research on the size of your potential market. You've secured rock-bottom prices from suppliers. You are extremely confident that you can make your business work. And then, the day after you open, a shop down the road starts selling flowers.

Here's another scenario: imagine you're the CEO of a global technology company and you're about to bring out a new tablet computer. Your business's entire earnings have been forecast on the basis of a successful launch of your new product. Then a rival gets their lawyers involved and claims your product infringes their patent. You have no choice but to quarantine your launch at a cost of millions.

No matter how big or small your business is the actions of your rivals can affect your ability to operate. So ask yourself what your rivals might do when you announce your new service/venture/product. Might they respond by cost-cutting, or by upping their marketing budget, or could they bad-mouth you to the press? One good way to anticipate what their move will be is to put yourself in their shoes: how would you react if your rival made the move you're thinking of?

It's often said that a nimble and agile new player in an industry can leapfrog over slow and satisfied established players, but it's also entirely possible that whatever you do will awaken their commercial instincts and it won't be long before you see them hit back.

Demand

This is one of the most common reasons why good business intentions come to nothing: entrepreneurs and CEOs massively overestimate the demand for their companies' services.

Demand can decrease for numerous reasons. It might be, as above, that a rival starts to offer something similar, or it might be that the market changes (think of trying to sell CDs in an MP3 market), or the economy falters and potential customers tighten their belts. Often, however, it's because companies launch products and services that simply aren't desired by enough people. And that's for the simple reason that those businesses don't bother to carry out extensive market research before they launch.

A lack of demand needn't always be fatal, as sometimes demand can be stimulated. The most common way of doing that is through marketing and PR, but you might also be able to whet potential customers' appetites by lowering price points or throwing in desirable extras.

Manpower

Finding the right person for the job isn't always easy. If it was, no company would pay eye-watering fees to recruitment agencies. Whether you're looking to employ a small team of aeronautical engineers in your new factory, an army of labourers to help you harvest your crops, or just one charismatic sales manager, you may well find that the skills you need are not available where or when you need them, or at a price you can afford.

I've seen too many business plans over the years where founders have said that, with investment from me, they intend to hire a brilliant marketing manager, or a CEO from a FTSE 250 company, or take on a new team in their factory, only to find that the people they need aren't willing to give up the safety of their old jobs to work on a new venture.

If your plans for future success rely on appointing key players or hiring a big team, then you need to start thinking now about exactly who those people will be, which companies you'll poach them from and what skills they'll need to have. Start trawling sites like LinkedIn, talking to contacts and taking potential candidates out for a coffee.

Legislation

Changes in legislation can wreak havoc with business plans. To give you a recent example, when VAT went up in 2011 from 17.5 per cent to 20 per cent, Bannatyne Fitness took the decision that – in uncertain economic times – this was a cost we could not risk passing on to our members. If you have a turnover of £100m, such a change in legislation would cost you £2.5m. That kind of figure won't just affect your profits, it will also have an impact on your ability to invest in the business.

Sometimes, however, the impact of legislation can be even more significant. If grants are withdrawn, or the boundaries to districts are redrawn, or a council changes colour at an election, all the plans you've made might have to be remade.

If your plans are dependent on a branch of government continuing to provide services, or make decisions as they have previously done, then your plans are vulnerable. Just imagine what could happen to a property developer if there was a big increase in stamp duty, or a hike in capital gains tax for second properties.

Money

Since the credit crunch of 2008, businesses of all sizes have found it harder to borrow money on reasonable and affordable terms. Some business owners have looked to put their own money into their companies, but when they've tried to remortgage their homes to do so they have found that their homes are worth less than they'd hoped. There can be no doubt that many businesses have struggled, and failed, in the past few years because money has become harder to get hold of.

The faster you need to get your hands on investment, the more vulnerable you'll be. It may well be that you'll need to pitch to many more banks and investors than you had planned to, and in the time it takes you to secure funding, the moment for success might pass.

Of course, if you are looking for investors to back you in difficult economic times, they will probably want a bigger slice of equity to compensate for the extra risk. If you're not prepared to negotiate, then that's another reason why your plans may not proceed as planned.

What really matters in this situation is how you respond. If you can't get hold of the investment you want, then you might be able to remodel your financials to take account of slower growth. You may have to reinvest every penny of profit to be able to expand, but that doesn't mean that your business won't eventually succeed.

You

This might not be what you want to hear, but sometimes the reason why plans don't work out is because the person driving the project is, well, not quite up to the job. If you don't have the skills, contacts or drive to push your business forward, it's entirely possible that the biggest threat to your business is *you*.

If you're not tough enough to go through some rough patches, or don't understand your budgets, or are too scared of your team to tell them that they're not delivering as expected, then it means that you need to make some changes. In *Dragons' Den*, we see plenty of pitches from engineers, inventors and artisans who are fantastically talented in their fields, but pretty rubbish at running a business. If that sounds like you, you can try delegating the tasks you're not qualified to do, get some training for the skills you need, or find a business partner who can run the business while you get on with the things you are good at.

One of the hardest lessons in business is that when the boss is the weak link, the business is always going to be in trouble.

QUESTION

Who do I know?

IT'S A CLICHÉ TO SAY THAT SUCCESS IN BUSINESS IS DOWN
to who you know, but I'm living proof that that's not
necessarily the case: when I started my first business – an ice-
cream van – my contacts book was the *Yellow Pages*. I didn't
know anyone useful, but after a few phone calls I soon found
out who supplied the cheapest ice creams, and I was up and
running. The point I want to get across before I go any further
is that if you don't know anyone useful, it doesn't mean you
can't succeed.

However, good contacts can – and do – make a difference in business. When transactions are conducted between
people who trust each other and understand each other's
needs, then you tend to get better deals that produce better
results. It's been noticeable how many people have come onto
Dragons' Den in the past few years who are just as interested in

getting a Dragon's influence as they are in getting investment.

It's pretty well recognised that a well-stocked phone book is as valuable to a business as a well-stocked warehouse. However, while businesses usually have comprehensive lists of every member of staff, or detailed records of stock, or balance sheets itemising every asset, very few people ever make a formal list of their contacts. This chapter is about doing just that – identifying, storing, protecting and maximising one of the most precious assets any business can have.

Why contacts matter

If a friend says, 'I really enjoyed this movie,' most people are far more likely to go and see that movie than if a film reviewer in a newspaper says exactly the same thing. If you need a plumber, you are far more likely to feel reassured that the guy fixing your toilet knows what he's doing if he was recommended by a neighbour. And if you're desperate to hire a key member of your team, asking your friends if they know someone suitable is likely to be much cheaper and quicker than going through the conventional recruitment process.

Of course, your contacts don't just recommend people and services to you, they can also recommend you to their contacts. The more people you know, the more likely it is that you will pick up the phone to someone who says, 'You don't know me, but I was given your number by so-and-so . . .'

Your contacts effectively give you eyes and ears into their offices and industries. If you want to know what's going on in another department, or get a perspective on a piece of news from a different industry, then the more contacts you have, the better and more reliable the information you'll be able to gather.

And if you want advice about a particular course of action, then a well-placed contact can give you a steer in the right direction. There really can't be much doubt: really good contacts help you run your business.

Making a list

It doesn't matter whether you store your contacts on a computer, a BlackBerry or a notebook, what matters is that they are stored in the place that is most useful for you. Start by gathering together all the different ways in which you access the names and numbers of people you know – computer records, email inboxes, your mobile phone, an old phone book, the Rolodex on your desk, your Facebook friends, your LinkedIn contacts and your old diaries that might have crucial phone numbers and addresses in them – and start methodically going through everyone you know.

And when I say everyone, I mean it. A contact isn't just a senior executive or someone with an impressive job title. Really well-connected people will make use of every contact they have, from the receptionist in a rival's building, to someone they remember from school. Even if someone you know isn't immediately 'useful' for your business or career, they still might know something that can help propel you forward. As you look at your contacts, it might help to ask the following questions about the names you come across:

- What do they do for a living?
- What have they previously done for a living?
- What are their hobbies and interests?

- Have they ever run their own business?

- What circles do they move in?

- Who do they know?

- Are they a potential client?

- Can they introduce me to potential customers?

This exercise should reveal that you are only a couple of phone calls or emails away from a vast and valuable world of information, recommendations and support. Someone you know probably already knows whatever you might need to find out. And if you need to find new customers or clients, these are the people you should look to for introductions.

Friends and acquaintances

I follow about 300 people on Twitter. They include some family members, a lot of the charities I have worked with, some celebrities I've become friends with, my fellow Dragons and most of the businesses I've invested in. I have an active interest in what all those people and organisations do, but that doesn't mean that I know them all particularly well – in fact, there are a few that I've never met. But they are all people I could tweet to find out a useful contact in their field, or to ask for their opinion.

The success of social networking sites like Twitter and Facebook has made many people realise that they are better connected than just their immediate circle of friends. In our day-to-day lives, we might only have a handful of people we see and speak to regularly, but online we might have thousands of friends. Which is great for business, because the most important contacts you'll have in your career are unlikely to be your closest friends. Usually, your close friends share your interests, live in the same area and have a similar outlook: that's why they're your close friends. But it's also what makes them less valuable as business contacts, because they know the same stuff you know, and the same people too: they can't tell you much you don't already know.

Conversely, the acquaintances you don't see very often because they work in a different department or a different continent will have a whole circle of contacts that you don't know. They're usually much more useful to you, especially when you need a fresh perspective. As you compile your new contacts list, scrutinise your distant contacts just as carefully as your closest colleagues and friends.

Who do you know of?

Once you've made a record of all the people you actually know, it's worth considering if people you haven't even met could be useful to your business. You might have read about them in a trade publication, or seen them speak at an event. As it's pretty easy to guess a lot of people's email addresses, it's not hard to make contact with total strangers. It's even easier to track people down on Twitter, LinkedIn and Facebook. And if that fails, a quick Google can reveal a person's contact details. A lot of the time, if you know *of* someone, you can find a way of contacting them, which means that it is possible to ask for advice or recommendations from a much wider circle. If, for example, you want to hire a patent lawyer and you've never hired one before, you could approach inventors and entrepreneurs you've read about and ask them if they would recommend their lawyers. Most people would respond to such a reasonable request, so when you start to compile a list of the people you know, spend some time thinking about the people you know *of*.

While you're looking at your contacts, it's always worth keeping the following question in the back of your mind: is there anyone you know who is so important or influential or possibly even rich that you should be tailoring your business (or at least your next week's work) around this individual? Do you know someone who, with one phone call or one purchase, could transform your business?

Maintain your contacts

Of course, now that you have your list of contacts, it's important that you maintain them: drop people an email, invite them out for a catch-up, or just follow them on Twitter or befriend them on Facebook. Your contacts book might not show up on your company's balance sheet, but it is nevertheless one of the most valuable assets you own. Which is why you should always, always, ALWAYS back it up. If it's on paper, photocopy it. If it's digital, store it in several places. If you lose your contacts, you're also bound to lose some business.

QUESTION

20

Who do I need to get to know?

NOW THAT YOU'VE WORKED OUT WHO YOU KNOW, IT'S A good time to work out who you don't know. There are certain people that everyone in business will need to know at some point in their career, and no one is going to get to retirement without needing a good lawyer, or a sharp accountant, or a spy in their rival's business. This chapter is about identifying the people you should be adding to your contacts book.

In your building

Let's start with the place where you work. Think about the people in your building who make the big decisions, appoint personnel, award contracts or allocate budgets. If you're not the boss, who is? (And perhaps more importantly, who's their PA?) Getting to know people at the top of your organisation is one of the best ways of making sure that you'll eventually join them. If you don't know your boss, think about ways you can get to know him or her. Can you send them regular updates about what your department is up to, or perhaps follow them on Twitter? Are there meetings you can volunteer to attend where you will get a chance to impress the top brass?

The senior people in your organisation aren't the only people you should be looking to get to know. Getting on well with the IT department is always a smart move, and in my experience, receptionists often know an awful lot of office gossip.

If you run a department, the best way of making sure that you are getting the right allocation of budgets and resources is to be able to pick up the phone and call your opposite number in another department, to check they're getting the same treatment. Spend some time methodically going through the people who work at your company and think about who it would be advantageous to get to know.

In your rivals' buildings

There are times when you need to work with your rivals – for instance, if you ever lobby for changes in legislation – and there are times when you want to inflict as much damage on their commercial chances as you can. Either way, when you know someone in a rival business well enough to pick up the phone, things have a habit of working out to your advantage.

If you're more than a couple of years into your career, there's a pretty good chance that one of your former colleagues now works for one of your rivals. If that's the case, drop them a line or take them out for a beer. If you've got an industry conference coming up, book your place and scour the delegates list for people you should be accidentally-on-purpose bumping into at the bar. And if you don't recognise the names on the delegates list, then buy a subscription to your industry's trade publication and look out for people who would be useful to you.

One of the most important reasons you should know the people who work for your rivals is that at some point in the future, either you will be hiring, or you will be looking to get hired. If you can talent-spot the people you want to employ, you will be strengthening your business. And if you can identify the people you want to work for, you can start to target them and their business.

Professionals

Having a good lawyer and accountant at the other end of the phone can save you a lot of time, and probably money. At some point in your career, you might also need to hire a PR agency, or a recruitment agency, or an architect, or a designer, or some other kind of professional. Even if you don't know these people directly, it's always good to get a personal recommendation, so think about who among your circle of contacts use these kinds of professional services and start compiling a list.

Advocates

When I tweet about something on Twitter, 400,000 people know about it instantly. When Stephen Fry tweets, over a million people know about it. If we recommend a product or service, it usually has a big and immediate impact. You need to identify the people who can recommend and endorse you to the biggest possible number of people. There might be a very influential blogger in your field, or a journalist for an important publication (and depending on your business, the most influential publication might be your local paper), or a dignitary or celebrity who can vouch for your skill/service/ product to their followers.

Legislators

Every successful career involves its fair share of bureaucracy. When I had an ice-cream van, I needed to comply with health and safety regulations; in my care home business, I had to be licensed by the local council; in my health club business, I need planning permission to build a new club. Believe me, it's all a lot easier to deal with if you have a good working relationship with the people and organisations that inspect, regulate and legislate for your industry.

In a government building somewhere near you is a person who can make your life easier or tougher, depending on how well you understand their requirements and how well they understand your business.

Future employers

Even if you currently run your own business, you might not always do so. Thinking about where you might want to work in the future and who will employ you makes a lot of sense, as does getting to know the top headhunters and recruitment professionals in your industry.

Customers

How can you get to know more of them? Think about where your customers hang out, and then think about how you can meet them. Are there websites you can monitor, Twitter accounts you can follow, Facebook groups you can start, or conferences you can attend?

You might have thousands of customers or just a handful, but if you can get to know a few of them personally, you can start to learn how they view your product/service/company. Instead of relying on focus groups and surveys, you can call them up and say, 'Did you notice we just launched X? What do you think of it?' It's always good to be able to see your business from your clients' perspective, and the more you know your customers, the more you'll understand your business.

QUESTION

What are my rivals up to?

RULE ONE: KNOW EVERYTHING GOING ON IN YOUR organisation. Rule Two: know everything going on in your rivals' operations. The more information you have on what your rivals are getting up to, the more you will be able to respond to whatever challenges they present.

I keep up to date on my rivals in the health club industry in a number of ways. I subscribe to every industry magazine and website. My team attends conferences and conventions. I have Google alerts for every operator, and every senior executive in those organisations. I follow key players on Twitter. I look at their share prices in the *FT*. If one of their members praises their service, or criticises it, anywhere online, I'll know about it within a few hours. And while some of my rivals probably wouldn't let me take out membership of their clubs, close friends and family are members, and they keep me informed of everything my rivals offer. In addition, I use mystery shoppers, who go into rivals' clubs and report back to me on everything from the cleanliness of their changing rooms, to the quality of their fitness instructions, to whether or not they could negotiate on joining fees or membership rates. I also study my rivals' published accounts.

Whether my rivals make money, appoint a new director, or introduce a new piece of fitness equipment, I make it my business to know about it. If I'm ever asked to go on *Celebrity Mastermind*, my specialist subject should be the UK health and fitness industry.

Whatever industry you're in, there will be similar tactics you can employ that will give you a really clear picture of what's going on inside your rivals' offices. And if you've been in your industry for a while, it's likely that you'll also have numerous personal contacts among former colleagues who now work for rival organisations. After a few beers, who knows might get revealed?

The sorts of things it's useful to know about your rivals include whether they're planning to:

- launch a new product
- expand into new territories
- hire new staff
- lay off staff
- drop/raise their prices
- bid for new contracts

But almost anything you find out about a rival can be used to your advantage. Whether it's the fact that the boss has sold her Bentley, or they've just placed a big order with a new supplier, they're all clues that give you an insight into how well their businesses are really doing.

Of course, everyone knows that everyone else is watching what they do, so a lot of the comments on Twitter or in the industry press are just puffed up (if not made up) pieces of PR designed to make you nervous/jealous/curious. The only way to really be sure how well your rivals are doing is to scrutinise their figures. If your rivals are publicly listed, everything from the CEO's salary to their turnover will be public knowledge, as it is a legal obligation to publish this information. Private companies have an obligation to lodge their yearly accounts with Companies House. The information they are legally bound to provide isn't as comprehensive, but it will still tell you what their turnover and profit is. Analysing your rivals' accounts is a really good way of checking whether the image they project is an accurate reflection of the state of their business.

It's also a useful tool for you to check how well your business is being run. You can see if your senior team is being paid the going rate, and you can measure your profit margin against your competitors'. What your rivals' balance sheets can also tell you is whether or not they are undervalued, or vulnerable to small changes in costs or tiny drops in profit: all very useful information if you are thinking of expanding. After all, one of the best ways to neutralise the threat a rival poses is to buy them!

What are my rivals' weaknesses?

ONE OF THE MOST IMPORTANT THINGS TO LOOK FOR when you scrutinise your rivals is where they have weaknesses. If you can work out where they are vulnerable, you can use that information to your advantage. It may help to turn back to Chapter 16 – What are my company's strengths and weaknesses? – and go through the exercise there again. However, this time do it from your rivals' perspectives. The results can be surprising, because the very qualities that your rivals would consider strengths can actually reveal potential opportunities for you. The classic example of this would be, say, a well-established company thinking their brand was valued by their customers, only for you to realise that their conservative, mainstream brand was actually vulnerable to the launch of a trendy, younger brand with contemporary values.

The big reason why this exercise is so valuable is that even if you only succeed in identifying your rivals' strengths, it still helps your company position itself in the market.

Differentiate yourself

Generally speaking, customers and clients make the decision to purchase a product or service based on four criteria: price, service, quality and convenience. Taking each category in turn, try to work out where your rivals let their customers down. Once you've identified their weaknesses, you've simultaneously identified the areas where you can compete.

Successful businesses work out where they sit in the market pecking order and play to their strengths. If we take an extreme example from the high street, Primark doesn't try to compete with Marks & Spencer on quality, but it has built a very successful operation by competing on price. In business, there's much less profit to be had from being a slightly inferior copy of an existing business than there is in offering a distinct identity to consumers. The best way to differentiate your business is to offer something that your rivals don't. If their customer service is crap, guess what? If you improve your customer service, you give their clients a brilliant reason to start using you instead.

Customers also make choices based on something intangible – brand. Branding is a complex and specialist subject worthy of a book (probably several) on its own, but the reason why it is so valuable is because it differentiates one offering from an otherwise similar offering. There are plenty of people who would rather buy a Sony TV than an LG TV with an identical spec, even if the LG model is significantly cheaper.

Similarly, some passengers would rather fly with Virgin, even though a number of other airlines fly the same routes, have the same safety record and probably offer slightly lower fares. And it doesn't seem to matter what tablet computers other manufacturers make, they will never be as cool as Apple's iPads. I mention this because it can sometimes be hard to see the difference between businesses that compete in the same industry: one accountancy firm is much like another to most people. If you struggle to find a major weakness, or a significant difference, between you and your rivals, then branding is one way of differentiating yourself.

Look beneath the surface

Your rivals' weaknesses might not be readily apparent, but if you keep digging you will eventually come across their Achilles' heel. I've already mentioned that I regularly look at my rivals' accounts, because it's a great place to find a business's hidden weaknesses. I look at their level of debt, the assets they own and the cash they have in the bank. If I see that a rival is heavily geared, I can probably predict they might have trouble getting new lending, or would be vulnerable to a big rise in interest rates. This can be valuable information: if I then plan a big marketing push at a time when I know they can't afford to respond, I can expect to do their revenues some damage while increasing my own.

There may be other weaknesses that it will take you time to uncover. Looking at their key members of staff can often reveal interesting insights. If a long-serving executive is due to retire, or if a family-owned business is prone to in-fighting, it's probable that your rival is about to go through a period of instability.

As I've already said, a strength can easily become a weakness: if your research shows that your rival's biggest asset happens to be a brilliant sales manager, then you can immediately create a weakness in your rival by poaching that sales manager. If you look for the opportunities where you can score points for yourself while causing pain for your rivals, you can make a really big impact on your company's future.

QUESTION 23

What do I waste time on?

SOME THINGS IN LIFE AREN'T FAIR. SOME PEOPLE ARE BORN to rich parents. Some people are dyslexic and find school difficult. Some people are better-looking than others. Some are born with a faulty gene. Some people are in the right place at the right time. However, there is one resource that is distributed fairly among the entire population of the planet – no matter whether you are rich or poor, young or old, the CEO or the gofer – and that is time. Every single one of us gets the standard allocation of 24 hours a day. Which means that what you do with your time can have a far bigger impact on your career than what you do with your money.

There are two ways you can waste time: you can spend years of your life pursuing unattainable goals, or you can lose two hours a day playing Angry Birds. I'm going to leave the big wrong job/project/relationship situations for the next chapter and focus for the time being on the day-to-day activities that eat time like a panda eats bamboo.

Traditionally, a working day has been about eight hours long, with an hour off in the middle for lunch. But of those seven hours of paid work, how many hours are you actually working for? It's a question that every employer wants to ask about his or her employees. When you see people gossiping in the kitchen, or updating Facebook, it's very easy to find yourself fuming, 'But I'm not paying you to do that!' One of the most alarming things I ever read was a report on something called the 'Efficiency in Business Survey' that was published in 2005. It discovered that the average office worker loses 48 minutes a day to technological failures (e.g. printers jamming and computers crashing) and an additional two hours a day in pointless meetings, or dealing with unnecessary phone calls or annoying colleagues. That's nearly three hours, or around 40 per cent of the working day!

However, I fully understand that only a robot can work solidly for eight hours a day. It took me a few years as an employer to realise that some of what I pay people to do cannot be measured or quantified. A few minutes spent talking about last night's TV, or finding out how someone's date went are actually a really important part of being in a team. And as teams almost always achieve more than individuals, those minutes spent gossiping by the kettle aren't wasted at all. But when people start spending hours gossiping rather than working, then you know you're in trouble.

As a business owner or manager, you're in a much better position to deal with any time-wasting habits your staff have if you've got your own habits under control first. As you carry on reading, think about how these suggestions apply both to you and to your team.

Keep a diary

This is always a really unpopular suggestion, but making a log of how you actually spend your day is a massively useful tool. I know why people don't want to do it: it's tedious, nerdy and they may well find out something about themselves they'd rather not know about. We all acknowledge that we spend some of our day making cups of tea, gossiping or surfing the web, but I think we're all a bit scared to face up to just how much of our day we waste. Which is precisely why this is such a good exercise to do. I could ask you to keep a diary for a week, or even a month, but I'll settle for just one day. It's usually enough.

From the moment you get up to the moment you go to bed tomorrow, keep a notepad (or an iPad) to hand and every 15 minutes log what you've just been doing. It's very easy when you do these kinds of exercises to forget, and you suddenly realise that you haven't written anything down for three hours, and you can't remember in enough detail exactly how long you spent queuing up for lunch, or responding to emails, and so the diary of your day is next to useless. You therefore need something that will remind you to make entries. Some people find putting their watch on the other wrist helpful – every time you go to check the time, you are reminded to make an entry. If there's something you look at several times a day – whether it's a clock on the wall, or a TV screen in the corner, or the door into your office – stick a Post-It on it to tell you to make a note. These prompts will help you make a more detailed time diary, and the more detail you end up with, the more useful it will be.

The following day, sit down with your activity log and see if you can spot any patterns. Do you, for instance, work better in the morning than the afternoon? Do you get more done when the office is empty? Do you spend too much time waiting for other people to get their work done? If so, these are all clues that can tell you where you should be making changes in your routine.

You can also see how much of your day is spent in meetings, or in transit, or on paperwork, or with clients, or supervising other members of your team. What will become clear is that some of your time is more productive than the rest. You may even feel that you earn all your salary in just a few hours a day: the key to growing your business, or racing up the career ladder, is to have as many of those productive hours in your day as possible. Once you can see where you are more productive, you can apply this information in other situations and start to make more of your hours more profitable.

There's another way of assessing productivity (and increasing motivation) that some self-employed people find really useful, and that's working out what their hourly rate is (there's no secret to it – just divide your annual income by the number of hours you work). Now, imagine that you could get your work done much faster if you stopped all your time-wasting habits. Your time log will show you how many hours you waste each day, so just deduct these wasted hours from your working hours and repeat your hourly-wage calculation: suddenly you are earning a lot more per hour.

If you can ditch the bad habits, you then have a choice: either take on more work and earn more money, or enjoy more time off.

Big time-wasters

A few years ago, I wrote a book called *How to Be Smart with Your Time*. While I was writing it, I came across all sorts of research on how inefficient businesses and individuals can be. So I want here to briefly run through some of the biggest time-wasters I came across.

Striving for perfection

It's very often the case that a piece of work can be carried out to a satisfactory standard in a reasonable amount of time (A). Carrying out the same piece of work to the highest of standards takes an unreasonable amount of time (B). If you think about how many hours you spend getting to A, and how many more you spend getting to B, you will see that the hours spent getting to A are significantly more profitable. In business, perfection is almost always a luxury that few clients or customers are willing to pay for.

Meetings

Most meetings are pointless. There, I said it. And I mean it. Before we even talk about what's on the agenda of your meetings, let's look at how much time (and maybe money) is spent getting to that meeting. Even if that meeting is taking place in your building, you will still stop working several minutes ahead of the meeting (or work less productively in the run-up to it), wait for ten minutes for the latecomers, listen to the points of view of several people who are irrelevant to the project, and then agree to reconvene in a week's time to discuss it further. Some people at that meeting might have also taken hours to get to it.

If that in any way sounds familiar, then pull out your diary, see how many meetings you've been to in the past year and have a stab at calculating how much time has been wasted. The next time someone asks you to a meeting, think hard if you really need to be there.

My rules for a successful meeting are really simple: there should be as few people in the room as possible, and the meeting should be as short as possible. All internal meetings I attend at our office last no more than 20 minutes. With such a tight deadline, people make their points quickly and concisely, and we can make decisions and move forward. I've noticed an increasing trend to have meetings standing up: while this isn't always ideal, it's a really good way to encourage participants to get to the point and keep things brief.

These days, so much can be achieved by copying relevant people into emails, or by video or phone conferencing, that an actual face-to-face meeting should only take place when it's strictly necessary. The more meetings I attend, the more meetings I vow to avoid in the future.

Commuting

Not only are commutes expensive, they can be demoralising and frustrating, as well as time-consuming. A tricky commute is no way to start your working day. Billions of hours that could be productive are sucked out of the economy by inefficient and tiring commutes. If you spend more than an hour a day getting to and from your place of work, I urge you to think if there's something you could do differently. Perhaps it would be possible to travel outside the rush hour, or work from home for some of the week, or maybe there's a different way to commute. Taking the train, for example, may take longer than driving, but if you can work on the train, it may improve your productivity.

Don't just look at your own commute: look at how everyone else in your building makes their way into work. If everyone in your building has a difficult commute because your office is somewhere with poor public transport, then maybe the next time your lease is up you should be thinking about moving.

Poor systems

Most people aren't very good at controlling their work flow. They leave things to the last minute, and then rush their work. Or they start something they really don't have the time for. The inevitable errors (because they rushed) create more work, and the people who were waiting on that piece of work to be completed before they can get on with their own work are left twiddling their thumbs. A really good project manager can save an organisation a lot of time, and therefore, an awful lot of money.

Poor motivation

The biggest reason why people don't work well and why projects take longer (and cost more) than they should is that the workers involved are poorly motivated. I don't mean that they are slackers or work-shy (although that may be the case); I mean that their boss hasn't motivated them properly to do their work. The biggest and best way to motivate a workforce isn't to pay them more (although that can help): it is to give them a reason to do a certain piece of work by a certain deadline. If they know that substandard or late work will create headaches for the rest of the company, the chances that they will deliver good work on time shoot up. Very often, clear communication about the importance of their work to co-workers or clients can produce dramatic results. If people understand how their work will be valued, they start to value it themselves.

Other ways to motivate teams including paying bonuses, or paying for a few treats if deadlines and standards are met. It doesn't always require money – sometimes simply praising people's work, or offering them opportunities for advancement gives them the motivation they need to work faster and better.

There may be other reasons why you or your team aren't working to your capacity – perhaps you haven't been given the resources to do the job well enough, or a detailed enough brief, or a meaningful deadline, and without these things, it's much harder to knuckle down and get the job done. If you suspect that you are in this position, ask your boss or your client for a better brief or a specific deadline, or to let you know how your work fits into the bigger picture.

Solutions

If you have identified that you or your team waste a lot of time on a daily basis, there are a number of things you can do. The first, and most important, is clearer communication about what exactly is required and when it is required by. The next thing is to improve the way you prioritise tasks, so that they get done in the right order. I have a really simple suggestion for how to do this:

- Grab a piece of paper and draw four columns on it.

- In the first column, make a 'to do' list of everything you and/or your team needs to do.

- In the second column, give every task a score out of five depending on how important it is (with five being for the most important tasks, and one for the least important).

- In the third column, give every task a score out of five depending on how urgent it is.

- In the fourth column, add up the two scores.

- Nine times out of ten, the task with the highest score is the one you should prioritise.

- The exception is when an unimportant task scores a five for urgency.

The other way in which you can transform your productivity and stop wasting the company's time is to get everyone on the team to play to their strengths. If you give an innumerate person the accounts to do, they will take much longer than someone who has a head for figures. Obviously you'd never be stupid enough to do that, but the point is that some people are naturally suited to certain tasks: the companies that find the best fit between the people they employ and the jobs they employ them to do are by far the most productive. If you find that you spend a lot of your day on particular tasks, ask yourself if this is because you aren't the best person to do those tasks. If you think someone else could do the job much quicker than you, then you should find a way of delegating it to that person.

QUESTION 24

What's not worth the effort?

THIS IS A BIT DIFFERENT FROM THE LAST CHAPTER, WHICH was all about reclaiming the minutes and hours that are frittered away by every business every day. In this chapter, I want to look at the projects that we might spend several months, or even years, on that are destined never to amount to much. Your business might be carrying legacy projects commissioned by people who no longer work in the organisation, or indulging in vanity projects that will only ever flatter the boss's ego rather than the company's balance sheet. This chapter is about identifying – and ditching – the projects that are diverting attention and funds from the activities that will really see your company thrive.

Before I do that, I need to issue a word of warning: earlier I talked about Google giving their engineers a day a week to experiment. There are plenty of other examples of businesses and individuals engaging in actions that while unlikely to lead directly to riches, are nevertheless an integral part of future development. A footballer, for example, needs to be fit in order to kick a ball in the 90th minute of a match. But – and this is the crucial part – there will come a point when any increase in the footballer's fitness will produce no additional benefit unless he has sufficient ability to pass or shoot. It's surprisingly easy to kid yourself that by doing the business equivalent of fitness training, you'll eventually be able to score goals. This chapter is about making sure you are not confusing being busy with making progress.

Heads, walls and banging

Ever heard the phrase that 'to do tomorrow what you did today and expect a different outcome is a sign of insanity'? It amazes me how many times people in business tell me that if they just keep doing what they've been doing, then they're bound to get the results in the end. The truth is, if what you're doing today isn't getting the results you desire, then there's really not that much hope that it'll get the results tomorrow. For outcomes to change, actions have to change first.

Let's say you've been trying to hire a particular calibre of candidate, but have consistently failed to do just that. Unless you change your approach, you are simply wasting time and money on advertising and recruitment agencies and interviewing candidates who are never going to come and work for you. Obviously there is a chance that the right candidate is out there somewhere, but there's a far greater chance that you're not able to hire the best candidates because they feel their ambitions can be better realised elsewhere. You need to accept that either your recruitment process isn't working, or the opportunity you are offering isn't good enough.

Here's another scenario. Your firm keeps bidding to win a contract from a particular client. Every year this client puts the contract out for tender, and every year you pitch for the business and fail. Clearly what you're offering isn't what they want. Or perhaps you have been training a member of staff for months to do your stocktaking, but they consistently fail to keep track of your stock. After that amount of time, the chances are that it's not the lack of training that's a problem: it's the member of staff. You should find something else for them to do.

Identifying that fine line between perseverance and insanity isn't easy. If you keep chipping away at something, you might eventually have a breakthrough, and that's why so many of us stick with things we probably should have abandoned long ago. Because it's hard to know when you've reached the line, it's sensible to draw your own line before you embark on a project. Let me explain: if you think a project is in danger of continuing without success for the foreseeable future, then you need to put an artificial limit on how much time, energy and funds you will let it take up. The way to stop wasting resources on a project is to decide in advance that the project will have a budget of X and a deadline of Y. If either of those lines is crossed, you stop what you're doing and move on to the next project.

Long shots

When your kids tell you that they want to be an astronaut, or a movie star, or the prime minister when they grow up, it's hard to know what to say: should you give them a big dose of reality, or should you let them hold on to their dreams? After all, every now and then, kids who work hard and have the talent do become astronauts, movie stars and prime ministers.

Human beings like long shots. We love seeing movies about underdogs slaying Goliath, we like hearing about authors who had their novel pulled off the slush pile, or a rookie coming on in the dying minutes of a match to score the winner. But just because long shots make good stories, it doesn't mean that they also make good business.

There's a phrase that every investor is very familiar with: the risk/reward ratio. In life, the reward of becoming an astronaut or a movie star is so great that the risk that you are unlikely to fulfil your ambition – no matter how brilliant, or talented, or even hard-working you are – means that it is worth striving for. It *could* be you. And that thought, that fantasy, will keep a lot of people reaching for the almost unattainable.

In business, however, the rewards are rarely that great. Mostly, you have the option of several courses of action: the first might be risk-free and produces a tiny profit; the second might involve an element of risk, but produces a decent profit; and the third is incredibly risky, and might just produce billion-pound revenues. In most cases, the sensible course of action is somewhere in the middle, because you have very little of the risk and enough of the reward. Most of the time, the long shot isn't your best bet.

If you look at the projects your company is working on at the moment, can you identify the long shots that aren't worth the risk? Could your team's efforts get more reliable rewards if you redeployed them elsewhere?

Just because

In every business, as in every family, you will do some things for the simple reason that you have always done them. Because the system/product/process worked in the past, you carry on with it in the present. You never question whether there is a better way of doing things, or even if the thing still needs to be done. Just like a parent cleaning a child's bedroom long after they've left home, you might be spending your time and effort on a job that no one cares about anymore. If you can identify the activities your company has been doing for a long time, there's a reasonable chance that you will find there is some fat to be trimmed and some slack to be tightened.

QUESTION

How big should my business be?

THIS IS A REALLY INTERESTING QUESTION TO ASK YOURSELF,
and you might be surprised at the answer. Very often, the act
of stating that you're going to be the biggest player on the
field is the catalyst for becoming just that. I don't think you
can underestimate how significant it was that, early on in his
career, Bill Gates shared his vision of there being a computer
on every desk in America, or that Mark Zuckerberg could see
that Facebook wasn't just for Harvard, it was for *everyone*.
Having a vision of where your company should be is a vital
first step in making sure that you, and it, reach your potential.
Of course, what the history books don't record are all the
other entrepreneurs who felt sure they were going to launch a
world-beater but ended up losing a fortune, and their reputation, in the process. Having a vision of global domination
doesn't guarantee you'll become a world-beater.

Comparing your business to something as massive as Microsoft or Facebook isn't necessarily helpful, but it's important to realise that every successful business had to start somewhere. Take John Griffin: he started his career as a taxi driver, but now runs the multi-million-pound Addison Lee cab company. Rod Aldridge started his career in the post room of his local council, and even though that sounds like a dead-end job, he ended up starting Capita, the biggest outsourcing company in Britain, and specialised in running council services. And then there's me: I could have stuck with one ice-cream van, but I eventually had a fleet of them. It's entirely possible for a small business to become a much bigger business: after all, if you can successfully run one ice-cream van, how hard can it be to run several?

Over the years, I have met people who have made immense fortunes from the exact same industries that other people have only made a living wage from. Some people own one buy-to-let property; some own hundreds. Some entrepreneurs open a corner shop; some start a chain of them. So, let's try to work out how big your business should be.

Big or boutique?

There are a handful of businesses where you have to be big to survive. Facebook is a brilliant example: it works best when the majority of people (at a university or within a social group), or a significant minority of the total population use it. Groupon is another example: they need hundreds of thousands of members in order to persuade clients to offer decent enough discounts for their members to take them up. Some businesses simply need scale in order to survive.

On the other hand, sometimes the old adage of 'if you can't beat 'em, don't even bother to join 'em' holds true. I'd say it's pretty much impossible for a new entrant to compete with the big venture capital firms, like 3i, to get a slice of major investment deals. So I don't. The other Dragons and I invest at the boutique end of the scale, putting in tens of thousands of pounds into businesses we care passionately about, rather than the billions 3i has to invest.

One of the best examples I can think of where the ambition and vision of the founder has influenced the size of the business is the clothing company Superdry. There are numerous manufacturers who produce casual wear for the surf dude market, and while many are household brands, none has achieved what Julian Dunkerton has with Superdry. Originally, Superdry clothes were sold through his chain of Cult clothing stores, but when the designs were so popular, he started selling them through other outlets. And then, to capitalise on the brand recognition, he started to open Superdry-branded shops all around the world. Then he opened up mega shops in prime retail locations. His next step was to float on the Stock Exchange for £400m. At one point, the business was valued at over £1bn. Dunkerton started boutique, but saw the potential to go big.

Great things in small packages

I was talking to an entrepreneur recently who told me he employs around 37,000 people. He has a billion-pound turnover and offices in ten cities. 'I really miss the days when it was just me and the original team,' he told me. 'The days when it went from four of us to about thirty were the most fun I've ever had. We all knew each other, we all cared about each other, and I think everyone cared about the business. These days I walk into our headquarters and the people on reception don't know who I am. I step into the lift and I never see a familiar face.'

I knew exactly what he was talking about. Small businesses are a lot of fun. That feeling of everyone pulling in the same direction and knowing everyone else in the building can be simultaneously rewarding and secure. If you love what you do, love the people you work with and love your business, there might well be a very powerful reason to limit the size of your business or slow down your rate of growth: you simply enjoy it more.

Other businesses simply cannot grow any bigger because they are limited by the capacity of the founders to expand. A freelance writer, for example, can only write so many articles a week, or books a year. They are hired because an editor admires their style, or their previous work: that freelancer can't outsource their work to another writer. If they are already working all the hours they can, the only way they can grow their business is by increasing the amount they charge, but there will be a limit to the premium any newspaper or magazine would pay, even for the best writers. That freelance writer can't scale up their business, and many other people – from landscape gardeners to wedding planners – will find themselves in a similar situation. Some businesses just don't have scale.

A natural size

For other businesses, there is a natural limit to how big they can grow, and that is usually governed by the size of the market. Bannatyne Fitness is actually a really good illustration of this. We currently have 61 clubs, and I would have thought that in five years' time – unless we acquire another chain of clubs, which is entirely possible – we will have a very similar number of branches.

That's because we have developed very specific criteria for locations in which we will open a new club. We have already opened a club in most of the locations that meet our criteria. In a handful of cases, we haven't built a Bannatyne's because one of our rivals has beaten us to it and there simply isn't enough of a market for both of us to survive. That means that Bannatyne Fitness has reached its natural size: we might close a couple of clubs, we might open the odd one, but for the foreseeable future, we won't be looking to expand.

I think it's really important for CEOs to have an idea of the natural size of their business. The example of RBS reminds us all that trying to become too big, too quickly can be disastrous. If you try to become something that the market can't sustain, you will putting unnecessary stress on your existing business – and possibly threatening its survival.

QUESTION 26

What are we getting right, what are we getting wrong?

THERE ARE TWO VERY GOOD REASONS FOR ASKING THESE two excellent questions: the first is that if you can work out what you are doing right, you might learn something that can be transferred to the rest of the business; and the second is that if you can identify what you are doing wrong, you can either ditch it or change it. Either way, this is an extremely valuable exercise, and not just for business owners – employees can learn a lot by rephrasing the questions to 'What am *I* getting right, what am *I* getting wrong?'

I have found that this is a really good subject to mull over when you're away from the office. In fact, the perspective you get from stepping away from the day to day can really help you see the answers to these questions more easily. So, imagine yourself on a lounger by the pool, the sun is shining, you have turned your phone off . . . now, what is your business getting right?

To help you get an even better perspective on what's really going on at your company, try to see your business (or yourself) from other people's points of view. For example:

What do your clients think of you?

Put yourself in your clients' shoes. If you were them, if you were paying what they're paying, would you be happy with the service or product you offer? Think about all the ways your clients interact with your company, and try to imagine how they view your business. Go through their contact with your firm step by step, and at each stage try to see things from their point of view, from the way they are treated when they arrive on your premises, to your invoicing and payment options. It might help to imagine a particular client, ideally your best client, and try to work out what their biggest gripe about dealing with your firm would be.

What do your employees think of you?

Now imagine that you are a member of your team. What do they think you are getting right? You can be pretty sure that they think you're not paying them enough, but what else would they be unhappy about? Think about the atmosphere in your building: is it a good place to work? Is the work rewarding? Are your staff given regular feedback on their work, or praised when they do their jobs well? What's your employee turnover like? If it's high, then you're doing something wrong. What might that be?

What do your rivals think of you?

This can be particularly illuminating. If your rivals were assessing your business, what would they think of your products and service? Which members of your team would they like to poach? If you come to the conclusion that there are aspects of your business that your rivals wouldn't envy or respect, what does that tell you about your business?

What do your shareholders think of you?

Mostly, of course, shareholders are interested in making a return on their investment. But they might nevertheless be worried that you are putting short-term gain ahead of long-term stability. Or that your expansion plans aren't ambitious enough, or too ambitious. What do they think of your top team? (By the way, even if you don't have shareholders, trying to see your company from an investor's point of view can bring a really helpful perspective.)

What do the press think of you?

Of course, it might be that the press have never heard of you and/or your business, in which case, one of the things you know you're getting wrong is your marketing. Perhaps you need to start writing articles for trade publications, or start a blog, or appear at industry events. Or maybe you've had bad press recently and certain moves have been misconstrued and your reputation has been tarnished. If that's the case, think about how you can redress this. Alternatively, you might come to the conclusion that you've been overexposed of late and need to lie low for a while. Mulling over these sorts of issues can help you time future media announcements for maximum benefit.

I encourage you to try to see your business through as many different lenses as possible, because the more perspective you gain, the more clearly you see yourself. The important thing to keep in mind as you sip on another papaya juice while lazing on your sun lounger is that uncovering your flaws is just as valuable as working out what your successes are. The more honest you are, the more you'll get out of this exercise.

QUESTION

Where will the industry be in ten years' time?

IF I COULD ACCURATELY PREDICT THE FUTURE, I WOULD BE a lot richer than I am! Let's face it, none of us really knows what lies ahead, but that doesn't mean that this exercise isn't extremely valuable. By making a judgement about what is *likely* to happen, or even about the general direction of travel, you can steer your business, and your career, on a better course through the years to come.

Specific predictions are rarely right, and when they are, it is probably the result of fluke rather than foresight, but general predictions about trends and markets can be really valuable. I can't tell you, for instance, how many books I will sell in ten years' time, but I can be pretty certain that I will sell more electronic copies of my books than paper copies, as there seems to be a very rapid transition towards e-readers. Obviously

151

predictions will vary from industry to industry, but I hope the suggestions below will help you plot a likely route forward.

Technology

I've already talked about the next technological shift to impact on your business, so I won't dwell on it here, but turning back to Chapter 5 might help spark some ideas of how new gadgets, or payment methods, or innovations like geolocation software might impact on your industry.

But I would also encourage you to think about other ways in which wider technological change could affect your industry. If we take social networking as an example, in a decade's time there will be millions more consumers around who grew up with Facebook and Google+. They will never have known anything but the era of social networking, so what does that mean for the ways in which you will interact with your future consumers? What will their expectations of customer service be? How quickly will they expect you to listen to their opinions and incorporate their feedback into your product or service? The chances are that every industry is going to have a much less passive relationship with their customers: how will that interaction affect what you do?

Technology is also changing our lifestyles: you can live in the Highlands of Scotland and still shop at Harvey Nics and read the *New York Times* every day. Skype and FaceTime mean we can have far more meaningful relationships with people we don't see very often, or possibly have never even met. How might these social changes impact on your industry?

More and more, technology is connecting individuals and bypassing intermediaries, whether that's authors uploading books directly to Amazon, or holidaymakers staying in a stranger's spare room thanks to Airbnb.com. What does this trend towards individualisation mean for your sector?

Globalisation

No matter what happens with the economy (see below), the chances are that globalisation will have a big impact on how we all run our businesses in the future. The internet means that consumers can compare prices of products from companies anywhere in the world. We might outsource our IT to India. We might recruit internationally. We might even be able to take a one-hour Virgin Galactic flight between London and Sydney. The chances are that in ten years' time, your firm will have more international customers, suppliers and enquiries: what does your business need to do to respond to this shift?

Demographics

Changes to the population – both nationally and internationally – may have an impact on the shape of your industry. It seems likely that for the next few decades, the population in the West will age and birth rates will fall, whereas in the Middle East, a higher proportion of its population will be under 25. Meanwhile, India is set to overtake China as the most populous nation on Earth. Are these shifts meaningful to your industry? Will there be greater profits to be made in new territories because of these changes?

Economics

It seems likely that the global economy is going to continue to be volatile as the West deals with its corporate, personal and sovereign debts. Does that create problems or opportunities for your industry? Should you be looking east in search of growth and profits?

When you try to predict what the economic landscape will look like in a decade, think about what might happen with regards to interest rates, inflation, taxation, oil prices and exchange rates. At the time of writing (early 2012), there is a lot of speculation about the future of the Euro: should you have a contingency plan in place in case the Euro breaks apart?

Consolidation

Entire industries often go through periods of consolidation, where one company buys another, merges with a third and then gets taken over by a fourth. In the past few decades, it has happened in industries as diverse as energy, cable TV, mobile telephony, health clubs and high-street banks: is your industry next? If so, which will be the companies to do the buying, and which companies will they try to buy? On which side of the fence is your business: should you be readying your balance sheet for a major purchase or bulking out your short-term profits to get a better selling price?

Growth v decline

Most industries, like economies, are cyclical. There are boom years and lean years. Sometimes, of course, industries never recover. I don't suppose we'll ever see TV rental companies come back onto the high street, or horse and cart deliveries make a comeback (unless, of course, something alarming happens to the price of oil). Which part of the cycle is your industry in? How best can you ride the wave of growth, or deal with a long, drawn-out decline?

As I said at the beginning, no one can accurately predict what the world will be like in ten years' time, but by looking at these kinds of areas, we can make a reasonable guess about where our industries are headed. While your forecasts may well prove to be inaccurate, the process of going through this kind of exercise can keep you alert to the opportunities and threats ahead.

QUESTION

What would a new owner do?

THIS IS A REALLY USEFUL QUESTION TO ASK YOURSELF.
Imagine that your business is taken over, and try to see it
through the new owner's eyes. A new owner would look to
cut out dead wood, save money and maximise revenues. Their
decisions would be made without sentimentality and without
any loyalty to your staff or your customers. The question you
need to ask yourself is: if someone else can make my business
more profitable, why can't I?

Reduce costs

The first thing a new owner would do would be to look at
your cost base and see where there are savings to be made. To
start with, take another look at Chapter 15 on wasting money,

and see if there are some obvious ways in which you are shelling out unnecessarily.

The next step is to look at any ongoing contracts you have with suppliers. If they haven't been renegotiated for a while, there's a reasonable chance that you are either paying for something you no longer need, or overpaying for a service you could get more cheaply elsewhere. You might also want to look again at internal contracts: are you paying too much, or being too generous with your benefits to staff? Perhaps more pertinently: do you have too many staff?

Why not ask every member of your team to suggest three ways in which the company could save money? Not only will they appreciate being asked for their opinion, but you can then implement the changes with their blessing. It's also entirely possible that they are aware of overspends that are easily hidden in monthly or quarterly accounts and that would never otherwise come to your attention.

Maximise revenues

While you're at it, why not ask your team for suggestions of ways in which you could bump up the bottom line? If your staff have a closer day-to-day relationship with your customers, they'll probably have some really valuable insights into additional products or services you could offer. To give you a really simple example, a few years ago, one of our receptionists at one of our health clubs told me that a member asked if we had any swimming goggles his son could use. We didn't, but we now have shops inside our clubs that sell an array of fitness accessories.

One of the most basic rules of business is that it is much

more cost-effective to retain existing customers than it is to go out and find new customers. If you can find more products or services to sell to your existing client base, then you can boost your revenues at very little cost. Just as a hairdresser tries to get his customers to have highlights as well as a trim (or at least buy some shampoo), think about the additional items or services you can sell to the customers you already have.

Selling assets

Asset-stripping is often controversial, but it can nevertheless be lucrative. If your business owns assets that it either doesn't need or isn't getting enough value from, then you might be able to boost your profits by selling them. These might be physical assets – like buildings – or they might be less tangible, like mailing lists.

If someone were to buy your business, they would get every asset you own independently valued. Every now and then, it's probably a very good idea that you do the same, because you might find something you can profit from. Perhaps a property has increased in value because of a change in planning regulations, or it might be that you no longer need your city-centre offices and could move your team to a cheaper space in the suburbs. Your company might own all sorts of assets – patents, prototypes, old stock, software licences, subsidiary businesses – that could all give your accounts a boost if they were sold at the right time.

However, I have a very serious word of warning about selling your assets for short-term gain at the expense of long-term success. Unlike our mythical new owner, who is only interested in maximising profits in the short term, you probably have long-term aspirations for your business. If you behave like an asset-stripper in search of a fast buck, you could be doing massive amounts of damage to your company.

Take the example of Southern Cross care homes. It was a business founded by one of my very best friends, a guy called John Moreton, and it was once one of the most successful chains of care homes in the UK. But then John sold the business to a consortium who sold the freeholds to their care homes for millions of pounds, and then rented the properties back from the new owners for tens of thousands of pounds.

In the short term, millions of pounds were returned to the company and distributed to directors and shareholders. But in 2011, the company started to hit the headlines: the property companies were putting up rents, and the public-sector cuts meant local authorities no longer had the same budgets for elderly care. Southern Cross couldn't pay its rent. The security of vulnerable residents was at risk, as were thousands of jobs. While the jobs were saved and no resident was made homeless, Southern Cross went bust. All because it had sold assets and the directors had taken profits out of the business.

The moral of the Southern Cross story is that if you are interested in what happens to your company in the future, be very careful about what assets you strip out of it in the short term.

QUESTION

How much is my business worth?

WHETHER OR NOT YOU PLAN TO SELL YOUR BUSINESS, IT'S very useful to have a rough idea of how much your business is worth. Of course, the true value of anything can only be determined when it is actually put up for sale in an open market, but regardless of whether you are thinking of selling up, making your own estimate each year gives you a sense of how much progress you're making, and where you sit in your industry's pecking order.

Anyone who's ever watched *Dragons' Den* will know that the best way to make a Dragon angry is to overvalue your business. I lost count several series ago of the number of deals that fell through because entrepreneurs thought their ideas, or their prototypes, were worth millions. The reason for this is that businesses are valued on the basis of their profits, which means low profits = a low valuation. After ten series, I hope Britain has finally got the message: an idea is not a business.

Some basic maths

In most situations, the valuation of a company is achieved by multiplying its profits by a specific figure called the 'multiple'. That multiple is usually the subject of debate, but there are a few guidelines that should be followed. The first is to look at the valuations of comparable publicly listed companies, and these are quoted in every edition of the *Financial Times*. If Company A operates in your industry and has a profit of £1m and a market capitalisation of £5m, then you could argue that the multiple that should be used to value your company is 5. If the multiple in your sector is 3, then you can triple your profits to come up with your valuation. Similarly, if it's 9, then you multiply by 9. Simple.

If there are no comparable publicly listed companies, then you need to find another way to calculate your own multiple. In most of the deals I have been involved in, the multiple has been somewhere between 2 and 8, but most often it's been between 3 and 5. As a general rule, the more established (i.e. the less risky) your business is, the higher your multiple will be. If you don't yet have a year's worth of accounts, you represent a very risky purchase, and therefore your multiple will be lower.

The multiple used for each industry changes over time. If your sector is in favour and is seen as the next big thing, then your multiple will be inflated. During the dotcom boom of 1999–2000, for instance, multiples of 40 were used (no wonder things went bust). It's unlikely we'll see those kinds of figures again, but it's still true that if you can demonstrate your business is on the verge of rapid growth, you'll be more likely to get a higher valuation from the market. Buyers get excited by growth, and a business with potential is a business with a higher price tag. It's only right: if next year's profits are going to be double last year's, valuing your business on the old figure would be unfair. Equally, if your sales are declining year on year, the multiple you would be offered for your valuation would be reduced.

Up for negotiation

In reality, business valuations are usually a bit more involved than doing a simple sum. Not only will sellers want to try to bump the price up by factoring additional assets into the sale, but buyers will dispute the value of those assets. A good example is property: a seller may run their business out of a valuable property, and that may be desirable to a buyer, but that won't necessarily be the case. In such a scenario, the seller would get a better price selling the property and the business separately.

The contents of your buildings are also considered assets, from the desks to the paperclips. Leftover stock can also be included in the sale, but the truth is that all these extras should be properly added to your profit and loss accounts, which means they already form part of your valuation because they have been included in the profit figure used in the multiple calculation.

Sometimes intangible assets like contracts, patents and copyrights are included in sale documentation, but unless the commercial application for these items is well-established, they are hard to value, which is why using profit is the fairest way of determining the value of a business.

There is one other 'asset' that sellers tend to think is much more valuable than buyers, and that's goodwill. Goodwill can be summed up as the difference in profit you would make if you started trading from scratch or if you bought your business and benefited from the ongoing relationship the previous owners had with their customers. A really simple example would be this: let's say you buy a high-street shop that is currently run as a dry-cleaner. If you continued to run it as a dry-cleaner, there is a very good chance that the previous owner's customers would become your customers, in which case you would benefit from the goodwill felt towards the previous owner. However, if you want to open a sandwich shop on those premises, then the goodwill of the dry-cleaning customers isn't worth a penny to you. To a certain extent, the value of the goodwill is dependent on the intentions of the buyer.

The final factor that can affect company valuations is timing: if you are selling in a buoyant market and can wait for your pick of purchasers, then your valuation is likely to be higher. But you should also always work out what your auction price would be: if you had to sell in a hurry, how much would you be likely to get for your business at auction? A business – like anything else – is only worth what someone is prepared to pay for it. If a buyer senses that you are desperate to make a sale, the chances are that they will bargain a lot harder to get you to drop your asking price.

QUESTION 30

Am I in the wrong job?

THERE'S A PRETTY GOOD CHANCE THAT THE ANSWER TO this question is 'yes'. Whether you are an employee or run your own business, circumstance probably means that somewhere down the line you took a job that you might not have meant to, and now you find yourself doing something that you're not entirely suited to.

The levels of 'misemployment' never show up in statistics, but I'd be willing to bet they're extremely high. The reasons why are obvious: most of us leave school without a clear idea of what we want to do, we end up taking a job because it pays rather than because it suits our skills, we slowly get promoted, and so ten years later we're working somewhere we could never have anticipated. Often, once you're in an organisation, you end up taking responsibility for certain functions because you happen to be in the meeting, or the boss couldn't hire the right candidate and asked you to hold the fort temporarily, and so slowly but surely many of us end up in jobs that we're not particularly suited to. This is almost always the case if it's a company you started yourself: at some point near the beginning, you would have done everything yourself, and you probably only ever handed over responsibility for some functions when you found the right specialist. That probably means you've been left with the jobs that no one else is good at, rather than the role you would excel at.

In 2000, Bill Gates surprised everyone when he announced that he was stepping down from being CEO of Microsoft after nearly two decades in the role. He wasn't stepping down to spend more time on the golf course, which is what you might expect a billionaire to do. Instead, he had created a new position at Microsoft for himself: Chief Software Architect. He had realised that, over the years, he had been taken further and further away from the day-to-day work that had led him to create Microsoft in the first place. His natural skills were on the technology side, and while he was no slouch on the business side, there were better administrators who could manage the day-to-day operations. If Bill Gates can be misemployed, then any of us can.

As companies grow and expand, they need a different set of skills to lead them. A classic example is that of Google. In 2001, the two twentysomething founders, Larry Page and Sergey Brin, realised they didn't have the clout with investors to make Google into one of the biggest companies on the planet. So they hired Eric Schmidt, an experienced executive from Sun Microsystems, to be their CEO. Ten years later, when Page and Brin were nearing 40 and had a vital decade of experience behind them, Page once again became the company's CEO, and Schmidt became Google's chairman.

I recognised a long time ago that my talents lie in starting and growing companies, rather than running them. So when Bannatyne Fitness became established, I appointed a managing director to run the company, and that freed me up to invest in new ventures, appear on TV and write books. Bannatyne Fitness is a much better company these days because my MD, now the chief executive, is better suited to the role than I am.

The boutique trap

One of the most common reasons an entrepreneur can find themselves in the wrong job is that they get stuck in the 'boutique trap'. Many businesses are started by one person working alone in a room, and usually grow quite happily to be a small team. But growing that boutique business into a really big business can only happen if the founder is willing to take a step back from the frontline and take on a more strategic role. More often than not, the founder brings in the most money to the business, so if they stop selling, or manufacturing, or inventing – i.e. the very skill that caused them to start the business in the first place – the company can have a massive drop in revenue.

Understandably, plenty of entrepreneurs don't want to take the risk, and so they carry on focusing on the day to day and never give themselves a chance to focus on the month-to-month and year-to-year priorities. Their fear of a short-term loss of revenue damages their long-term earning potential. If you don't have any time for planning or thinking, then there's a pretty good chance that you need to change your job description.

Right person, right job

When we do jobs we aren't particularly suited to, we don't work to the best of our abilities, our output tails off (both in quantity and quality) and the business suffers (as does our morale). The most successful companies are those where the people who work for them have roles they were born to do. When you find that match between ability and opportunity, it is remarkable what can be achieved.

So although you might love your job – even if you are really well paid, even it's your business – it's always worth asking yourself if your current role makes the most of your talents. Could you make more of a contribution to the company in a different role? Is there someone in your organisation who is better suited to your job? These are questions that are very rarely asked, but if you don't ask them, you might never realise that there is a better way of running your organisation.

Obviously, if you're an employee and you think you're in the wrong job, you might not have the same scope for creating your ideal role, but there may still be ways in which you can get the job you want, whether it's renegotiating your terms and conditions with your boss, volunteering for projects that better suit your skills, or empowering co-workers to take on the tasks to which you are not suited. Of course, you might also find you can better fulfil your potential in another organisation.

QUESTION

31

Am I kidding myself?

THERE HAVE BEEN SEVERAL OCCASIONS DURING THE filming of *Dragons' Den* when we have had to tell an entrepreneur that the business they have devoted so much of their life, energy and money to is destined to failure. It's never a nice thing to say to someone, but the thing I've noticed is that the people who need to hear it the most are the people least willing to listen. I reckon that, more often than not, hearing a Dragon tear their business plan to shreds makes people say, 'I'll show you; I'll prove you wrong.' Instead of leaving the studio and reconsidering their business, they go straight back to the office and head even faster in the wrong direction.

I understand why, I really do. When you have put so much of yourself into a venture, and when the failure of that business means a loss of face and status, as well as money, then I completely get why some people refuse to see sense. It's the same for employees who hang around in jobs they don't much like because they think they're due a promotion, even though they keep being overlooked. I want to scream at them: 'Take the hint, you're not what your bosses are looking for, you're not valued where you are.'

Sometimes the reason why people don't realise their venture is doomed is not because they are short-sighted, nor is it because they are stupid, or lazy, or egotistical; it is just because they have been so damn busy. They've been working flat out for so long that they've never noticed that the demand isn't there, or that a rival has launched, or that the market has changed. When you work 16 hours a day, it's really easy to lose focus on the things that matter: I've known countless entrepreneurs who were working so hard that they didn't see something wasn't working until it was too late. So while I fully understand that asking if you're kidding yourself can be very painful, I also believe it actually protects you from something far more painful – and that's failure. Everyone's situation will be different, but here are a few suggestions for assessing whether or not you're following the wrong path:

Go back to the beginning

Go back to either your original business plan or your contract of employment and see how close you are to delivering what was promised. The closer you remain to your original vision, the more of your targets you have hit along the way, the more likely it is that you're on the right path.

When was the last time something changed?

Remember the saying that doing the same thing tomorrow as you did today and expecting a different result is a form of madness? If you've been plugging away at something for years, expecting your sales to soar, your clients to praise you, or your boss to pay your more, but these things haven't happened, the chances are they will never happen unless you make some changes of your own first. Unless you make those changes, you'll eventually have to accept that you are almost certainly kidding yourself.

Are you earning enough money?

This is a very blunt way of working out if it's time you should be doing something else, but if your income, or your company's profit, isn't sufficient to cover your costs, then you need to face up to the fact that you are very likely to be in denial about your prospects.

Who's better than you?

If there's a guy at the next desk who can do your job just as well in half the time, I can guarantee you that you won't get the promotion on offer. It's the same for businesses too: if another company can do what you do cheaper or better, then you are probably kidding yourself.

It's never nice to admit you're wrong, but it's a much better option than spending more of your life on a venture that is doomed. And when I say 'spending your life' what I really mean is 'wasting your life'. Do yourself a favour: be honest. If something isn't working out now, then at the very least, force yourself to come up with five good reasons why it might work in the future. If you can't come up with those reasons, you really, truly have to walk away.

QUESTION

What's the worst that could happen?

THIS IS THE KIND OF QUESTION THAT REALLY SUCCESSFUL companies ask. If you can have a contingency for any of the disasters that might happen in the future, then what might otherwise be a crisis can simply be downgraded to a bad day.

I would imagine that most people's first answer to this question would be something along the lines of the office burning down, or a strike shutting down production, but it's not always the big events that have the biggest impact. There are plenty of seemingly innocuous things that can do a lot of damage to a business. For instance, I was in the car the other day and I heard a phone-in on the radio about parental leave. A small business owner called in: he had five members of staff, four of whom had recently announced they were pregnant. He was beside himself: he couldn't possibly recruit four replacements in such a short space of time, he was worried about the cost of paying maternity benefits and scared that with four key people absent, clients would drift away and his company would fall apart.

The worst thing that could happen to your business will depend on the industry you're in. I'm sure BP and Shell have entire departments that prepare contingencies and damage-limitation programmes in the event of an oil spill. Just as I'm sure Hovis have watertight supply deals for flour in the event of a drought, or a flood, or a spike in wheat prices. Your industry will have similar specific threats: give some thought to what they might be, and then work out measures you could take to lessen their impact.

Every year, there are stories in the news about, for instance, car parts manufacturers that go bust when big car plants move overseas, or suppliers that are hit when retailers like Woolworths go bust. If you have a client that is responsible for a large percentage of your earnings, then you absolutely need to consider how you would survive if they went under. The best move in that situation would be to secure a broader range of clients.

I'm pretty sure that my businesses are relatively secure. We have regular turnover that far exceeds our costs and thousands of satisfied customers. So what do I worry about? Well, we have a lot of debt, so a big rise in interest rates would hurt us. We also have a hard-won reputation for delivering excellent facilities: I'd worry about an incident that called that into question, like – God forbid – someone drowning in one of our swimming pools. There are also a few key members of staff that I would find it difficult to replace.

Because I have worked out what the worst case scenarios for my business are, I have taken action to prevent them.

I have, for instance, made sure that the interest rate on our lending is either fixed or subject to a 'cap and collar' deal: it doesn't matter how much the Bank of England base rate goes up by, because my arrangement with the bank means it can't be passed on to us. Equally, I am rigorous about our health and safety training, and make sure that our staff know exactly what to do if someone gets into difficulty in the pool, and that members understand that they enter the pool at their own risk. And I protect the company from losing key members of staff by a) rewarding and incentivising them properly, and b) taking out something called 'key man' insurance should they find themselves under a bus.

Working out the worst thing that can happen means you can put contingencies in place. If your greatest fear is that your client ends a contract, make sure that your contracts have three- or six-month notice periods to give you time to find replacement clients. If your greatest fear is a rival opening up next door, then the best way you can prevent that is by deterring them by being the best at what you do. If you are reliant on a particular raw material, then get your orders in well in advance. If a strike would see you go out of business, then you need to negotiate with your workers.

This exercise needn't take up a great deal of time because, after all, the chances of these things happening are relatively slim. But as they can be extremely costly when they do happen, it's advisable to have some kind of contingency plan in place. After all, anticipating disasters is often the best way of avoiding them.

QUESTION

33

When should I leave?

THIS IS ACTUALLY ONE OF THE HARDEST THINGS TO GET right in business, but the issue of succession is really important for the health – and wealth – of businesses, as well as other sorts of organisations. Political parties that have been dominated by a charismatic leader for a decade will frequently find their leader's demise is followed by a period of turmoil in which several leaders fail in quick succession. That's because it's very often the fact that having one person in charge for so long causes damage: the whole organisation has become moulded to one person's preferences, and when that person leaves, the organisation has to be rebuilt. Which is why identifying a successor long before you intend to step down (see Chapter 2) can give you the confidence to step aside when the time comes.

It's also difficult for employees to know when to leave: if

they enjoy their work and are rewarded for their talents, it's possible to stay in a job too long. Eventually, complacency sets in, and resentment from other workers looking to move up the career ladder starts to seep out.

Whether you're an owner or an employee, timing your exit can have a massive influence on your career, *and* on the business you leave behind.

Advice for owners

I've lost count of the number of times I've heard an entrepreneur tell me that they love the business they started like a child. They have put so much of themselves into the business, and its success is so central to their sense of themselves, that the bond between a business and its owner is incredibly powerful.

I understand why many entrepreneurs think that no one on Earth could run their company, or care about their company, in the way that they do. But what they fail to see is that 'their way' certainly isn't the only way, and as a consequence, many business owners stay around long after an employee doing the same job would have been given a golden handshake and asked to make way for the next generation.

There are many examples of business owners who have stayed too long in their jobs, probably to the detriment of their companies. In 2011, there was a lot of speculation that the mighty Rupert Murdoch's decision-making had lost some of its commercial bite, and there was criticism of his handling of the phone hacking scandal. Murdoch faced a vote of confidence at a meeting of shareholders who wanted him replaced as chairman. He survived the vote, but the chance that one of Murdoch's children will eventually take over the running of the business subsequently seemed less likely. The verdict was that the business had outgrown the family.

My view is that if you love your business like a child, then the best you can hope for your business is that it will grow up to be a decent, prudent, self-sufficient entity that can stand on its own two feet. After all, that's all any of us want for our kids. There comes a point when a business, like a child, needs to know it can make its own way in the world without the indulgence of its owner to keep it afloat, or to make unreasonable demands on it.

Many founders become too protective of their businesses. They don't want to leave the balance sheet bare, so they don't invest the company's money on innovation in the way a new CEO probably would. They become increasingly conservative, and shy away from the kinds of risks that might damage their precious baby. The problem is that it is precisely those risks that allow businesses to grow. Bringing in new people with fresh ideas and the desire to make a name for themselves is the best way of making sure your business continues to thrive.

Timing isn't the only issue to consider: *how* you leave is just as important. Some founders move into the role of chairman of the board, either in an executive or non-executive capacity; some become a board member; others settle for being a major (and often that means majority) shareholder. On the one hand, the new team might find it handy to have you around for advice, but on the other hand, your presence may stop them from making changes out of deference. There are plenty of examples of 'retired' CEOs meddling and undermining from the sidelines.

A clean break is often best for both parties: the new boss can take charge, while the founder can concentrate on their next venture. However, if you intend to hang around, setting out a clear chain of command is essential, as is creating a formal framework for making contributions and suggestions.

Advice for employees

There are many good reasons why employees look to move on from their current role: promotion, recognition, money, experience, a fresh challenge, a better work/life balance, a more inspirational boss.

The average Briton will hold around eight to ten different positions in their career, from school to retirement. If you take your working life to be roughly 40 years, then that means the average time spent in any one job is four to five years. In some industries, it's not unusual to have 20 different jobs. What this means is that an individual job isn't as important as an entire career. So when you start to think that you want to move on, the important question you need to ask isn't 'Is this a better job?' – it's 'Is this the right move for my career?'

Career progression is based on three key elements: experience, skill and the ability to manage either people, budgets or data. If you're not getting a chance to learn these skills in your current job, then leaving for a position that will give you that chance is almost certainly going to be good for your career.

QUESTION

Am I too emotionally involved?

YOU DON'T HAVE TO BE THE FOUNDER OF A COMPANY to be emotionally involved in its success. Let's face it, most people spend five out of seven days at work every week. When you throw in a commute and the distinct possibility that there will be reports and background material to be read at home, our jobs take up a large part of our waking lives. Now add the fact that some of the best friendships will be made at work, that our salaries pay for our homes and help us provide for our families and that work represents not just what we do but very often who we are, it's not an overstatement to say that most of us really do care about our jobs, our colleagues and our companies. To a greater or lesser extent, we are all emotionally involved in our jobs.

Being emotionally involved is good for business. If we personally benefit from the success of a deal, then we are more likely to work hard to see that the deal is a success. If we didn't care about whether or not our company will still be in business in a week's time, then we would find it very hard to do our work.

Sometimes, however, emotional involvement can cloud our judgement, and as the best business decisions are made with the head, not the heart, when that happens we are no longer acting in the best interests of the company. If you're not sure where the best place to draw the line between healthy involvement and unhelpful fanaticism is, then perhaps the questions below will help.

Q1: Imagine you have been working with Jane for 15 years. She has been instrumental in growing the company, but now the company is established and her development role is no longer required. Her skills aren't suited to another role within the company. Would you find it impossible to make such a loyal employee redundant?

Q2: You hear a rumour that a rival company is bidding for a contract. Does this mean that you automatically feel compelled to bid for that contract too?

Q3: You are diagnosed with an illness and your doctor says that you need total rest and relaxation for three months. Would you find it difficult to hand over the reins to someone else for that time? Might you still call up every day 'just to see how things are going'?

Q4: A customer makes a complaint. They say your product or service is substandard. Is your first reaction that your customer is wrong?

Q5: You receive an offer to buy the business. It's more than fair at slightly more than the going rate. Do you instantly dismiss the idea of selling?

Q6: You read in the paper a positive story about your rival. Do you call up the journalist and tell them why they are wrong?

If you have answered yes to any of the above, then I reckon there's a fair chance that your judgement is clouded by your emotional involvement. There are some steps you can take to bring a bit more balance to your decision-making.

- Be a bit more democratic. Instead of taking decisions on your own, put them to a vote within your office, or at the next board meeting. By inviting other people to give their points of view, you might well see that your own point of view subtly changes.

- Delegate. There's a good chance you are too involved in details that really shouldn't concern you. If you can ditch some of the unimportant tasks, then you free up some space in your brain to make better decisions. Have a look at your workload and see if there are some areas of operation that you can let someone else get on with. If you are a control freak, then you won't find this easy, but if you start with more trivial tasks, you can slowly build up to more important activities. The secret to good delegation is to follow three straightforward steps: 1) fully brief the person you are delegating to on what you expect, 2) give them a budget and a deadline, and

3) let them get on with it. How they achieve the target you set them isn't important, so long as they meet it.

- Use an outside consultant. If you are too close to your company to see it clearly, the perspective an outsider brings could be extremely valuable to you. You don't have to abide by their decision, but if their thinking is different from yours, then this is maybe an indication that you are no longer thinking clearly.

QUESTION

What am I afraid of?

I THINK MOST PEOPLE HAVE A FEAR OF FAILURE. FOR some, the fear is so great that they will never start a business, just in case they lose their money or their dignity. For others, that same fear is the motor that drives their ambition and ensures their success. Learning how to use your fears can make a big difference in business.

I have a sneaking suspicion that the fears that keep us awake at night aren't the ones we should be the most afraid of. It's the little day-to-day terrors that should worry us more, as they inhibit our behaviour and lead us to make poor decisions. Things like a fear of picking up the phone, or a fear of confronting an employee's poor performance, or of looking at our accounts in case they tell us something we'd rather remain ignorant of. The problem with these daily fears is that, over the years, we subconsciously develop avoidance techniques, or coping mechanisms, so that we don't have to face them. It may be that you don't even realise you're afraid anymore, and are therefore completely oblivious to the ways in which your fears blight your career. The first thing, then, is to identify these hidden fears. Here are a few suggestions:

- We all know the physical signs of fear: a racing heart, sweaty palms, a dry mouth, a need to rush to the loo, falling over your words, a desire to run away. Think about the time you last felt any of these symptoms: they almost certainly indicate a secret fear. (If you can't think of a time, then look out for these symptoms in the weeks ahead.)

- Most of us have a 'to do' list somewhere, whether it's formally written down or just in our heads. Think about the tasks on your list, and then think about the tasks you've been putting off the longest. The chances are that the things you've been avoiding are the things you are a teeny bit afraid of.

- Look back to Chapter 16, which was about identifying your weaknesses. There's a pretty good probability that the things you aren't good at are the things you are afraid to tackle, just as a dyslexic person dreads being given background material to read.

Over the years, I have come across people who are scared of public speaking, making a phone call, going to meetings, going to the pub after work, meeting new people, arguments, negotiations, balance sheets and reading reports. All of which, I think you'd agree, are important elements in anyone's career.

Once you've identified your fears, it's possible to do something about them. My attitude is always to tackle things like this head on, or 'feel the fear and do it anyway'. I used to be absolutely terrified when I was asked to speak in public. I could barely get the words out, my throat was so tight. However, I knew that if I always turned down the chance to speak, I wouldn't gain the profile and influence I sought. So I made myself do it, and I slowly got better at it. These days, I don't just enjoy it, but people in the audience tell me they do too.

I think looking at the big picture can really help in these sorts of situations: if your fears are preventing you from achieving your long-term goals, then the discomfort in the short term is easily outweighed by the benefits over time if you conquer them. Putting your fears into perspective allows you to tackle them, and by and large, once you've tackled them a few times, they tend not to bother you again. They're like school bullies: stand up to them and they'll leave you alone.

QUESTION

Who are the rising stars?

THERE ARE MANY THINGS BUSINESSES CAN LEARN FROM sport: practice makes perfect, reading your opponent, having a game plan, getting in position, seizing chances, teamwork. These concepts have all turned up in countless business books over the years, but the one thing the business world hasn't imported from the world of sport is the concept of the talent scout.

Every Sunday morning, scouts from professional football clubs stand on the sidelines at school and junior league matches, looking for the next Rooney or Ronaldo. There isn't the equivalent in business. While some industries – notably pharmaceuticals and computing – have good contacts with leading universities in order to recruit specialists, most industries let new entrants come to them. In doing so, they fail to nab the brightest and the best for their own businesses.

Just as a football team needs to find teenagers to replace experienced players heading towards retirement, a business needs to find a constant supply of new employees, if only to keep your existing employees on their toes. There are huge benefits to having a workforce that spans the generations, primarily because that helps you tailor your goods and services to the widest possible demographic.

Needless to say, those companies that recruit the best talent will tend to do better than those that don't. While a few large corporations can still afford to fund graduate schemes, most small and medium enterprises simply do not have the resources to train people who may not end up working in their company long term. So how can you find and recruit the next generation of business stars to your organisation?

Your own back yard

Just like Dorothy in *The Wizard of Oz*, before you go looking for rising stars elsewhere, why not start in your own back yard? You might have some future leaders already working for you. If you employ the right talent-spotting systems, you can make sure that the really talented people in your organisation get fast-tracked to the top. This information may be readily available to you in your sales data, or you may have an Employee of the Month scheme, where the entire workforce can nominate a colleague. You might also have data available from HR that can tell you who gained ten GCSEs, or a first from university, which can be helpful if academic ability is central to what your business does. You can also ask for feedback from your customers as to which of your employees they've appreciated dealing with, or ask department managers who they would recommend for a bonus. You should use this information to identify and then observe the people who stand out.

Annual away days or Christmas parties are good ways to observe people in your organisation who you might not normally meet, and if you take part in them, you have a chance to get closer to your team and observe them in a different environment. Perhaps you could also have a 'welcome day' for new recruits, and try to meet as many of them as possible. Once you start to identify the future stars, invite them to your office, or take a few of them out for lunch. There's nothing like lunch with the boss to make an ambitious young professional feel that they're working for the right company.

Finding them elsewhere

It makes sense to hire the brightest and the best for two reasons: 1) they boost your business, and 2) it means your rivals can't employ them. And if they are already working for a rival, then poaching the talent hurts your rival while giving you a commercial advantage. So how do you go about identifying the workers with real potential when they don't work for you?

Your industry's trade journals can be a really good source of intelligence. Not only do they occasionally run features along the lines of '30 under 30', where a panel of your peers will have named the rising stars for you, but if you read the papers regularly, you will see news items and stories on people throughout your industry. If the same names keep cropping up, then perhaps you should take notice. Why not call them up, or get a head-hunter to do so, and invite them out for a coffee?

Tell your HR department, or an external recruitment consultant, that you want to know if a particularly well-qualified candidate sends in their CV, regardless of whether or not you have a vacancy advertised. If the right person comes along, you might just be able to create a role for them somewhere in your organisation.

Retaining them

The problem with really good workers is that, mostly, they know they're really good. They expect to be rewarded for their brilliance with money, accolades, opportunities and fresh challenges. That means devising bonus or incentive schemes to stop them going and working for someone else. Not everyone is motivated by money; for some, simply knowing that the boss appreciates and values their contribution is enough.

If you think you have a young professional on your team who could one day be an industry leader, start thinking now about how you can hold on to their talent and make sure they are still working for you in the years to come.

QUESTION

What am I doing tomorrow?

RIGHT. IT'S 9 A.M. IT'S THE START OF A NEW DAY. WHAT'S on your agenda? You've just read a couple of hundred pages of suggestions that will improve your business, so what are you going to tackle first?

In my experience, it's easy to hear good advice and never get round to implementing it, because as soon as you get back to work, the phone rings, or the photocopier breaks down, or you get pulled into a meeting. Suddenly it's two days later, or two weeks later, and the things you meant to change are still unchanged.

I have found the only way to get things done is to make a list. At the end of every day, or every meeting, I create a list of the actions I need to take, the people I need to call, the decisions I need to make. And throughout each working day, whenever I get a minute, I work through that list. And then I make the next day's list. If you make a list right now of the things from this book that you need to implement, the next time you sit down at your desk, you will be able to start making a real difference to your organisation, and to your career prospects.

Step 1: Make a list.

Step 2: Make some changes.

Step 3: Make more money.